Boardroom Cybersecurity

A Director's Guide to Mastering Cybersecurity Fundamentals

Dan Weis

Apress®

Boardroom Cybersecurity: A Director's Guide to Mastering Cybersecurity Fundamentals

Dan Weis
Melbourne, VIC, Australia

ISBN-13 (pbk): 979-8-8688-0784-8   ISBN-13 (electronic): 979-8-8688-0785-5
https://doi.org/10.1007/979-8-8688-0785-5

Managing Director, Apress Media LLC: Welmoed Spahr
Acquisitions Editor: Susan McDermott
Development Editor: Laura Berendson
Project Manager: Jessica Vakili

Cover designed by eStudioCalamar

Distributed to the book trade worldwide by Springer Science+Business Media New York, 1 NY Plaza, New York, NY 10004. Phone 1-800-SPRINGER, fax (201) 348-4505, e-mail orders-ny@ springer-sbm.com, or visit www.springeronline.com. Apress Media, LLC is a California LLC and the sole member (owner) is Springer Science + Business Media Finance Inc (SSBM Finance Inc). SSBM Finance Inc is a **Delaware** corporation.

For information on translations, please e-mail booktranslations@springernature.com; for reprint, paperback, or audio rights, please e-mail bookpermissions@springernature.com.

Apress titles may be purchased in bulk for academic, corporate, or promotional use. eBook versions and licenses are also available for most titles. For more information, reference our Print and eBook Bulk Sales web page at http://www.apress.com/bulk-sales.

Any source code or other supplementary material referenced by the author in this book is available to readers on the Github repository: https://github.com/Apress/Boardroom Cybersecurity. For more detailed information, please visit https://www.apress.com/gp/ services/source-code.

If disposing of this product, please recycle the paper

Table of Contents

About the Author and why this book

Dan Weis is the Penetration Testing Practice Lead at Nexon Asia Pacific. Dan has over 30 years' experience in IT, in a range of different industries, and was one of the first ten people in the world to become a Certified Ethical Hacker.

Dan also has over 18.5+ years of cybersecurity, management & consulting, penetration testing, and red team experience, with attributed zero-day vulnerabilities in SCADA/Control Systems software. Dan heads Up Nexon's team of cybersecurity experts, leading red and blue teams on offensive and defensive cyber operations to proactively assess company and government networks to increase their security posture and not become the next "headline."

Earning the nickname "The General" as a result of his multitude of industry qualifications, Daniel also holds an additional 22 industry certifications. In his spare time, Daniel undertakes research on the cybercrime underground, facilitates training sessions for budding ethical hackers, is a regular on the speaker circuit presenting on all things InfoSec and dark web, and has presented at over 80 conferences and events over the last five years.

Dan also has made appearances on television and radio and has a number of published resources, including books, magazine articles, newspaper appearances, online posts, and YouTube videos, and is an active participant in a variety of renowned security and industry programs. Dan has authored the book *Hack Proof Yourself! The essential guide for securing your digital world* and coauthored the book *Learn Social Engineering* that has received BookAuthority's Best Books of All Time award.

Preface

My name is **Dan Weis**, and thanks for picking up my book. I've been in the IT industry since 1994, and specifically in the Cybersecurity space for Over 18 years, performing penetration testing, vCISO services, security consulting, incident response, security auditing, and security training. I hold a multitude of certifications and have spent many years on the speaker circuit educating people and organizations on cybersecurity, cyber risk and resilience, the dark web, hacking and penetration testing, security awareness, as well as TV, radio, newspaper, and online resources. I breathe information security, and I love educating people and organizations to ensure that they don't become the next headline. We have enough issues to deal with in the world, without being hacked or beached as one of them.

I present to directors, boards, and organizations nearly every week on these topics, and the overwhelming feedback I get from most directors and boards is that they just don't understand cyber, cyber risks, pentests, audits, compliance, all these security areas where information is presented to them, and they need to try and decipher it to make decisions for the organization (and to obtain assurance) and also how this translates back to their obligations and requirements as directors. Because of this knowledge gap, all the information they receive is filtered because they don't understand the concepts, so the C-suite could be painting any picture for the organization and the directors would have no idea; by the same token the IT manager, as an example, might be requesting a large amount of capital for certain cybersecurity technologies that may not even reduce the overall risk profile for the organization.

My goal with this book is to empower you with the knowledge that you need as directors and leaders to navigate the complex world of cybersecurity, to ask the right questions from both internal and external stakeholders, and to ensure your organization is as cyber-resilient as possible.

Introduction

The digital age has ignited a new era of opportunity and efficiency. However, this interconnected world has also created a rapidly evolving landscape of cyber threats. In 2023 alone, cybercrime caused an estimated $6 trillion in global damages, a staggering figure that showcases the immense financial risk organizations face today [1].

This book delves into the critical realm of cybersecurity, specifically focusing on the ever-present threats that can cripple any organization. We will dissect real-world attack methods and mitigation strategies, analyze industry and regulatory requirements as they impact your boardroom decisions, and expose the vulnerabilities that leave organizations susceptible to data breaches.

But why should cybersecurity be a top priority for CEOs, directors, and board members? A successful cyberattack can be catastrophic. Beyond financial losses, data breaches can erode customer trust, damage brand reputation, disrupt critical operations, and even lead to legal ramifications for the board and for directors, such as regulatory fines and lawsuits.

This book empowers you to make informed decisions for your organization regarding cyber risk. We will equip you to not only understand the evolving threat landscape and the potential impact of an attack but also to proactively reduce and mitigate those risks. This knowledge will ensure you fulfill your reporting obligations and demonstrate strong corporate governance in the face of ever-present cyber threats.

The digital age presents immense opportunities, but it also demands a heightened awareness of cybersecurity risks. This book is your road map to navigating this complex landscape, understanding your obligations as a director or board member, and ensuring your organization remains secure and thrives in this increasingly digital world.

How to Use This Book

This book is broken down into two parts.

Chapters	Part
1–5	Part 1 – Understanding the Cybersecurity Landscape: Threats, Roles, Governance, and Frameworks
6–9	Part 2 – Overseeing Cyber Risk: Requirements, Attack Vectors, and Mitigation Controls

Each chapter ends with a "Key Takeaways" section to reinforce understanding of important concepts as well as a set of key questions for stakeholders.

Appendix

At the end of the book, you will find an appendix listing AICD, ACSC, and other cyber risk resources that can be referenced to increase understanding.

Glossary

Security and technology glossaries are provided at the end of the book that can be leveraged to look up key terms and definitions.

Index

An index can be found at the end of this book.

References

[1]   https://cybersecurityventures.com/cybercrime-
      damages-6-trillion-by-2021/

PART I

Understanding the Cyber Security Landscape: Threats, Roles, Governance and Frameworks

CHAPTER 1

The Evolving Threat Landscape: Understanding Cyber Threats in the Digital Age

The digital age has transformed how organizations operate, creating new opportunities for growth and efficiency. However, this interconnected world has also opened doors for malicious actors, leading to a constantly evolving landscape of cyber threats. In this chapter, we will explore the current and emerging threats that organizations face today, equipping you with the knowledge to protect your valuable assets and ensure business continuity.

© The Editor(s) (if applicable) and The Author(s),
under exclusive license to APress Media, LLC, part of Springer Nature 2024
D. Weis, *Boardroom Cybersecurity*, https://doi.org/10.1007/979-8-8688-0785-5_1

1.1 Traditional Threats with a Modern Twist

Although cybercrime tactics continue to evolve, some established threats remain a significant and ongoing concern for organizations; these include

Malware: Malicious software, including worms and ransomware, continues to plague organizations. Ransomware attacks, in particular, have become increasingly sophisticated over the years, encrypting critical data and demanding exorbitant ransoms for decryption.

Social Engineering Attacks: Social engineering attacks such as phishing and vishing aim to trick users into revealing sensitive information or taking an action, such as clicking malicious links or providing an access point into an organization. Phishing attacks continue to increase in sophistication daily along with business email compromise attacks (BEC) that target specific individuals within organizations.

The Human Element: The Insider Threat: Cyber threats don't always come from external sources. Disgruntled employees (malicious insiders), contractors, or even business partners can pose a significant risk. Typically, insider attacks are orchestrated by employees, often someone who feels they were mistreated, for example, they have been missed for that big promotion they had their heart set on, or someone who has been engaged by a competitor for competitive advantage. There are a number of cases where employees accept a role at another organization which is a competitor, and within their notice period, they exfiltrate data or sabotage the current employer to further enhance the competitor's position.

Typically, insider threats can involve stealing data, sabotaging systems, or inadvertently introducing malware through negligence.

Organizations need to implement robust access controls and security awareness training to mitigate insider threats.

Denial-of-Service (DoS) Attacks: These attacks overwhelm a website or server with traffic, rendering it inaccessible to legitimate users. DoS attacks can cripple online services and disrupt critical operations.

Traditional Network-Layer Attacks: Attacks exploiting vulnerabilities in systems or wired/wireless networks leveraging exploits.

Man-in-the-Middle (MitM) Attacks: MitM or interception attacks involving "sniffing" or sitting between two parties to intercept sensitive information.

Cryptojacking: This involves using a victim's computer to mine cryptocurrency without their knowledge or consent. Cryptojacking can significantly drain resources and impact system performance.

1.2 The Rise of New Threats

As technology advances, so do cybercriminals' techniques. The following are some emerging threats that organizations should be aware of:

Supply Chain Attacks: Although these attacks have been happening since as far back as 2007, they were few and far between and not widely publicized. With the massive increases in supply chain attacks over the past two years, I would treat these attacks as a new threat and attack vector that all organizations now need to consider. Cybercriminals are increasingly targeting third-party vendors and suppliers to gain access to an organization's network. These vulnerable areas are usually linked to vendors with poor security practices, which makes it crucial to assess the cybersecurity posture of your entire supply chain. Recent examples include the SolarWinds Attack (2020), the Kaseya Supply Chain Attack (2021), the MOVEit Software Attack (2023), the Okta Supply Chain Attack, and many more [2][3][4].

Internet of Things (IoT) Vulnerabilities: The growing number of interconnected devices within the IoT world creates new attack surfaces. These devices are often poorly secured, making them prime targets for cybercriminals to gain access to a network.

The Weaponization of Artificial Intelligence (AI): AI has taken the world by storm and is creating challenges due to the pace and speed of change and adoption. While AI holds the potential to enhance security measures (e.g., it is currently being used by security operation centers (SOCs) to identify threats and breaches faster), it is also actively being used by malicious actors to launch more complex and targeted attacks. AI-powered tools can be used to automate attacks, personalize phishing attempts, and even bypass traditional security measures. Current AI attacks are also being used to generate sophisticated voice and video recordings, imitating individuals, and are used in social engineering attacks.

An example of this is deepfakes [5][6]. Attacks using deepfakes and AI increased by 700% between 2022 and 2023, according to the *Wall Street Journal*. When a *Wall Street Journal* reporter experimented with an AI-generated version of herself, she was able to trick Chase's system [7].

AI and deepfakes are also being used in other ways to influence world events, for example, in fake election videos, and were utilized during the war in Ukraine by Russia, to disseminate misinformation [8]. Current trends see these attacks targeting individuals within organizations to facilitate payments to attackers.

Cloud Security Risks: Businesses are increasingly relying on cloud-based storage and services. However, cloud environments can be vulnerable to cyberattacks if not properly secured. Organizations need to understand the shared responsibility model of cloud security.

Cyberwarfare and State-Sponsored Attacks: Exacerbated by current conflicts, cyberwarfare is a growing threat. Nation-state actors are deploying sophisticated attacks for espionage, misinformation, disruption, and critical infrastructure sabotage, raising the specter of widespread damage.

As you can see, cyber threats are constantly evolving with new tactics and vulnerabilities emerging all the time. Constant vigilance is key.

Understanding current and emerging cyber threats is crucial for organizations in today's digital age. By being aware of the risks and implementing robust security measures, you can significantly reduce your organization's vulnerability to cyberattacks and protect your assets and data.

1.3 Key Questions for Your Organization

- Do we understand the current cyber threats our organization faces, both traditional (e.g., malware, phishing, DoS, supply chain attacks, cloud security risks) and emerging (e.g., IoT vulnerabilities, AI-powered attacks)?

- Are we regularly updated on the evolving threat landscape and the potential impact of these threats on our organization?

- Do we have a process in place to assess and prioritize these threats based on their potential impact on our operations, finances, and reputation?

- Have we assessed our vulnerability and implemented robust security measures to protect against traditional threats like malware, phishing, and denial-of-service (DoS) attacks?

- Have we assessed our vulnerability to emerging threats like supply chain attacks, IoT vulnerabilities, and AI-powered attacks?

- Are we implementing appropriate security measures to address these emerging threats, such as supply chain security assessments, securing IoT devices and AI-powered threat detection tools?

- Are we regularly reviewing and updating these measures to keep pace with the evolving tactics used by attackers?

- Are we staying informed about the latest developments in the threat landscape and adjusting our security strategy accordingly?

- Have we considered the risk of insider threats and do we have a plan in place to address insider threats from disgruntled employees or negligent individuals? This could include access controls, monitoring, and behavioral analytics.

- Are we monitoring user activity and implementing security measures to detect and prevent unauthorized access or data exfiltration?

- Are we regularly assessing and updating our understanding of the evolving threat landscape through threat intelligence and security awareness training?

- Are we educating our employees about these threats and providing training on how to identify and avoid them?

1.4 Key Takeaways

- **Cyber Threats Are Constantly Evolving:** New tactics and vulnerabilities emerge all the time, requiring ongoing vigilance and consistent education and awareness.

- **Traditional Threats Remain Significant:** Malware, social engineering, DoS attacks, and network vulnerabilities are still major concerns.

- **New Threats Require Attention:** Supply chain attacks, IoT vulnerabilities, AI-powered attacks, cloud security risks, and cyberwarfare pose growing dangers.

- **The Human Element Is Critical:** Insider threats from disgruntled employees or negligent individuals can cause extensive damage. Lack of awareness and training can lead to increased risks via human-based attacks such as social engineering.

- **Understanding the Threat Landscape Is Crucial:** By being aware of the current and emerging risks, directors can ask effective questions and make informed decisions about cybersecurity measures.

- **Robust Security Measures Are Essential:** Organizations need to implement strong defenses to protect their assets and data.

Having explored the ever-present cyber threats in this chapter, Chapter 2 dives deeper into the malicious actors' arsenal. We'll dissect real-world attack methods, analyze how organizations can implement effective defenses, and equip you to build a robust cyber defense strategy. The subsequent chapters will delve deeper into specific threats, explore best practices, and explain compliance and board responsibilities, empowering you to navigate this complex landscape.

Empowered by an understanding of these threats, directors can fulfill their cybersecurity oversight duties and make informed decisions that safeguard the organization.

References

[2]   https://en.wikipedia.org/wiki/Supply_chain_attack

[3]   www.upguard.com/blog/supply-chain-attack

[4]   https://cyberint.com/blog/research/recent-supply-chain-attacks-examined/

[5]   www.dhs.gov/sites/default/files/publications/increasing_threats_of_deepfake_identities_0.pdf

[6]   www.fortinet.com/resources/cyberglossary/deepfake

[7]   www.wsj.com/articles/i-cloned-myself-with-ai-she-fooled-my-bank-and-my-family-356bd1a3

[8]   www.cnbc.com/2024/04/08/state-backed-cyberattacks-ai-deepfakes-top-uk-election-cyber-risks.html

CHAPTER 2

Understanding the Who and Why

It's important for directors and board members to understand the motives and threat actors behind cyberattacks. It's big business and the third-largest economy in the world. A 2023 report by Cybersecurity Magazine [9] estimated that cybercrime caused $6 trillion in global damages and is expected to cost $9.5 trillion by the end of 2024 [10]. A recent report from the World Economic Forum anticipates the costs to climb higher, exceeding $23.84 trillion by 2027 [11].

Cybercriminals launch attacks for a variety of reasons, often categorized by the desired outcome. The following is a breakdown of some common motives behind cyberattacks:

Financial Gain

This is the most prevalent motive. Cybercriminals aim to steal money directly from individuals or organizations through various techniques:

Financial Account Takeover: Hacking into bank accounts or obtaining credit card information to steal funds (think AI and deepfakes)

Ransomware: Encrypting critical data and demanding a ransom payment for decryption

Extortion Attacks: Often used in conjunction with ransomware attacks, extortion attacks are leveraged against an organization once their data has been stolen (or exfiltrated) during a cyberattack. Some attacks are specifically designed to steal data for this reason; others are daisy-chained with other attacks such as data breaches and ransomware.

Data Theft and Espionage: Stealing sensitive information for various purposes such as

- **Identity Theft:** Using stolen personal information (e.g., tax file numbers and personally identifiable information (PII)) to commit fraud or open new accounts in the victim's name.

- **Corporate Espionage:** Stealing trade secrets, intellectual property, or confidential business information from competitors.

- **Extortion Attacks:** Same as financial gain above.

- **State-Sponsored Attacks:** Foreign governments may launch cyberattacks to steal classified information or disrupt critical infrastructure or to spread misinformation campaigns.

Disruption and Sabotage: Aiming to disrupt operations or damage a target organization's reputation, including

- **Denial-of-Service (DoS) Attacks:** Overwhelming a website or server with traffic, making it inaccessible to legitimate users.

- **Hacktivism:** Using cyberattacks to promote a political or social agenda. Hacktivists are individuals or groups who use cyberattacks to promote a particular social or political cause, which can damage an organization's reputation and disrupt operations.

- **Destructive Attacks:** Disrupting critical infrastructure or causing physical damage by manipulating control systems (rare but impactful).

Personal Vendetta: Carrying out cyberattacks out of spite or revenge against a specific person or organization. This could involve disgruntled employees, former business partners, or even competitors.

It's important to note that some attackers may have more sophisticated goals beyond these immediate disruptions. Advanced Persistent threats (APTs) are attackers who meticulously plan and execute intrusions to steal sensitive data over a long period, often remaining undetected for months or even years.

Thrill-Seeking and Notoriety: Some attackers are motivated by the challenge and excitement of breaking into computer systems and gaining unauthorized access. They may also seek notoriety by publicizing their actions online.

It's important to note that motives can overlap. For example, an attacker might launch a ransomware attack for financial gain but also steal data during the process to potentially sell it on the black market or extort the organization.

In addition, **the threat landscape is continually evolving:** Attackers are constantly developing new techniques to exploit vulnerabilities. This includes emerging technologies like artificial intelligence (AI) and Internet of Things (IoT) devices. Social engineering tactics also consistently become more sophisticated, preying on human emotions and trust. Adding to this complexity is the rise of supply chain attacks, where attackers target vulnerabilities in third-party vendors and suppliers to gain access to an organization's network.

Other considerations as to why an organization may be targeted include

Data They Are Holding: The more valuable the data, the more likely they are to be targeted.

Financial Interests and Assets: Larger companies can often pay ransoms as opposed to smaller organizations.

How Public Facing They Are: If an organization is often in the public domain and is high profile and well known, the more likely they would be to pay ransoms and extortions.

Political, Conflicts, Type of Organization, and Other Interests: For example, anti-abortion activists targeting a new abortion clinic, pro-Israel supporters targeting Hamas, etc.

Partner Organization Is Breached: An organization (outside of your control) is breached who held some data (even just emails) from your organization. Attackers then target your organization as part of the wider exposed data set.

Low-Hanging Fruit: Your organization may be classified as low-hanging fruit; that is, you may have a lower level of security maturity compared to other organizations. Attacks can often be opportunistic, and attackers are always after the path of least resistance. If you are running known insecure or legacy systems, the more risk-exposed the organization will be to cyberattacks.

Nation-State Attacks: In addition to the motivations listed above, nation-states can also launch cyberattacks for various reasons, including stealing classified information, disrupting critical infrastructure (such as power grids or communication systems), or sowing discord. Organizations that support critical national infrastructure, such as energy or telecommunication companies, may be particularly at risk from these types of attacks.

Insider Threats: It's important to note that while the focus of this chapter is on external attacks, organizations are also vulnerable to threats from within. Insider threats can arise from disgruntled employees, contractors, or even business partners who have authorized access to an organization's systems and data. These individuals may intentionally steal or misuse data or accidentally cause breaches through negligence.

The cyber threat landscape is constantly evolving, attackers are adept at exploiting vulnerabilities in emerging technologies like AI and IoT devices, and social engineering tactics continue to grow in sophistication, preying on human emotions and trust. Staying vigilant requires continuous learning about these evolving threats and updating security measures to stay ahead of the curve.

By understanding the different motives behind cyberattacks, organizations can better anticipate threats and implement security measures that address these specific risks.

So now that we have discussed the motives, let's discuss the methods.

2.1 The Typical Methods Employed by Cybercriminal Gangs

Cybercrime groups/gangs (think organized crime) account for the majority of cyberattacks targeting organizations today. Cybercrime groups/gangs are also referred to as cybercrime "families"; there are lots of them, and a lot of these families are connected in various ways (similar to the old mafia crime families).

Attackers (in particular cybercrime gangs) have a standard format or approach to breaching organizations and monetizing the breach. At a very high level, it looks like this:

1. Attackers target and breach an organization through the methods described in the previous chapters, typically via social engineering or phishing, compromising of weak user account passwords, exploiting of vulnerabilities, or access via supply chain attacks. They then ensure persistency in the network via stealth techniques to hide their presence and are typically in the organization's networks anywhere from days to months depending on the level of detection abilities for the organization and the sophistication of the gangs' tools and TTPs (Techniques, Tactics, and Procedures). If we take the Medibank 2023 breach as an example, attackers were in the network for months.

2. They start accessing and exfiltrating as much data as possible, such as financial or customer data and health records (basically whatever they can get their hands on).

3. Ransomware is then deployed within the network.

4. The CEO or senior management team member is
    contacted by what's referred to as a "negotiator"
    with the goal to cause panic and to threaten
    the organization with the release of data if their
    demands are not met.

5. At this point, a small snippet of data may be posted
    to darknet forums and/or to the CEO (or contact) as
    proof of the breach and access to data.

6. Attackers then put a timeline in play; for example,
    you need to pay x number of dollars, in 24 hours, 48
    hours, etc., or we will release the data.

7. If the demands are not met (and often, even if they
    are met), the cybercrime gang still releases the data.
    Some groups are true to their word and may release
    the data back to the organization only, but more
    often than not, these groups cannot be trusted,
    which is why the advice from both government and
    industry is to never pay a ransom or demand.

These cybercrime groups sell Cybercrime-as-a-Service (CaaS),
consisting of Ransomware-as-a-Service (RaaS) and Extortion-as-a-Service
(EaaS). The cybercrime groups provide all necessary services such as the
ransomware and other malware, the coders, the infrastructure to support
the operations, and the call center (support services).

This is then hired out by what's referred to as an "affiliate" (paid for via Bitcoin or another electronic currency), who are basically hackers for hire that buy into the CaaS solution, similar to a franchise, renting the ransomware/malware and infrastructure. They are also provided access to dark web resources facilitated by the gang to leak information as an example of proof of access.

The affiliate is the person who will facilitate initial access to the target; their job is to establish the entry point.

Once the affiliate obtains access, they then hand over to other teams provided by the cybercrime group, such as the offensive team, who take over after initial access and exfiltrate the companies' data, and the negotiators, who will liaise with the target to extort them of as much money as possible.

Other services such as Human Resources (HR) and coders are also provided by the cybercrime gang. The affiliate then receives a cut of the total profit made by the cybercrime gang.

The following figure shows a useful diagram to explain the breakdown of groups.

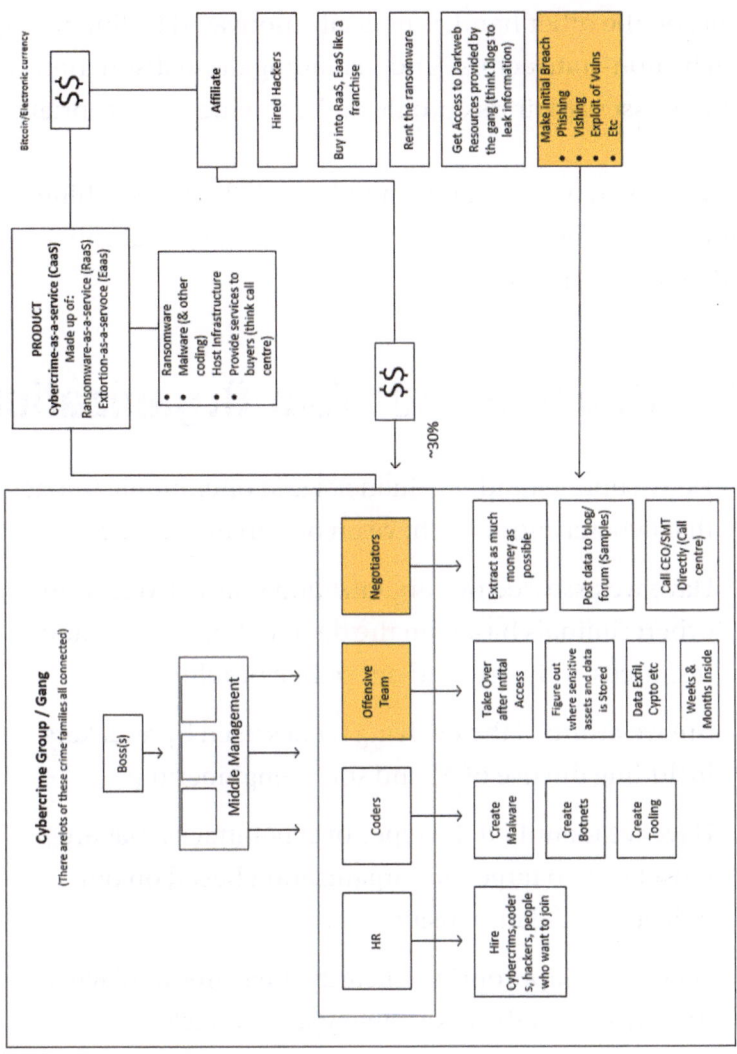

As you can see, it's a complex and sophisticated system that has many resources involved and moving parts.

A Quick Note on Cyberwarfare vs. Traditional Cybercrime

It's important to distinguish between cyberwarfare and traditional cybercrime. Cyberwarfare involves state-sponsored attacks targeting a nation's critical infrastructure for strategic objectives. Traditional cybercrime, on the other hand, is typically motivated by financial gain or disruption by non-state actors. Understanding these distinctions helps organizations assess their risk profile and implement appropriate security measures.

So now that you have an understanding of who is launching the attacks, their motivations, and the type of attacks, let's talk about organizational responsibilities.

2.2 Key Questions for Your Organization

- Do we understand the financial and operational impact that cybercrime could have on our organization?

- Have we assessed our organization's attractiveness to cybercriminals based on the data we hold, our financial resources, industry, and our public profile?

- Are we aware of the evolving tactics used by attackers, including the use of AI and social engineering?

- Have we identified the types of cyberattacks that are most likely to target our organization based on our industry and data sensitivity?

- Do we have appropriate security measures in place to defend against these specific types of attacks?

- Are we regularly reviewing and updating our security measures to address emerging threats and vulnerabilities?

- Have we considered the different types of threat actors that might target our organization, including cybercriminal gangs, hacktivists, and potentially even nation-states?

- Do we understand the motivations behind these different threat actors and how they might approach attacking our organization?

- Are we promoting a culture of cybersecurity awareness among our employees and board members?

- Do we have regular training programs and communication initiatives in place to educate staff about cyber threats and best practices?

- Are we actively monitoring and responding to cybersecurity incidents to minimize their impact and learn from them?

- Are we continuously educating ourselves about the evolving tactics used by cybercriminals through threat intelligence and security awareness training?

2.3 Key Takeaways

- Cybercrime costs trillions and targets all industries. Understanding attacker motives helps organizations to prioritize security investments.

- Attackers seek financial gain, data theft, or disruption. Advanced groups (APTs) can remain undetected for long periods within an organization's systems.

- Organizations are targeted for valuable data, financial resources, or as a result of weak security practices.

- Directors need to be aware of evolving threats and what action is required to protect their organization's critical assets.

- The cyber threat landscape is constantly evolving, and attackers are adept at exploiting vulnerabilities in emerging technologies like AI and IoT devices.

- Social engineering tactics continue to grow in sophistication, preying on human emotions and trust.

- Directors must not have the mindset that any business is immune to cyberattacks. While smaller organizations may underestimate their vulnerability, insider threats and ease of targeting make them attractive targets for attackers.

- Staying vigilant requires continuous learning about these evolving threats and reviewing and updating security measures to stay ahead of the curve.

References

[9]   https://cybersecurityventures.com/hackerpocalypse-cybercrime-report-2016/

[10]   https://cybersecurityventures.com/cybercrime-to-cost-the-world-8-trillion-annually-in-2023/

[11]   www.weforum.org/agenda/2024/01/cybersecurity-cybercrime-system-safety/

CHAPTER 3

Director Responsibilities and Obligations

Directors play a proactive role in fostering a strong cybersecurity culture within their organizations. This entails going beyond simply complying with regulations and taking a leadership role in prioritizing cybersecurity efforts. By demonstrating a commitment to cybersecurity from the board level, directors can set the tone for the entire organization and encourage a culture of security awareness among employees.

There are many different preparedness and reporting obligations required from organizations and boards. These will fluctuate based on the industry your organization operates in. For example, if you are in financial services, you will have APRA requirements; if you are classified as critical infrastructure, you must comply with the CIRM program requirements, etc.

A great resource that breaks down the obligations for organizations based on industry can be found here: `www.cisc.gov.au/resources-subsite/Documents/overview-cyber-security-obligations-corporate-leaders.pdf`.

In general, the following sections explain the preparedness and responding obligations that apply to the majority of organizations.

3.1 Australian Privacy Principles (APP 11) [12]

Australian Privacy Principles (APP 11) applies to an "agency" or "organization" within the meaning of the Privacy Act 1988 (Cth).

APP 11 requires entities to take reasonable steps to ensure the security of personal information held and to actively consider whether it is permitted to retain personal information. "Reasonable steps" are circumstance specific, but it is expected that you regularly review and assess the data you hold about individuals, including the sensitivity of the information and amount of information held, assess and implement security measures to protect the data (and determine if the measures themselves are privacy invasive), and adhere to data management requirements, such as destruction of data after a period, and de-identifying or anonymizing data. It is expected that organizations also assess the potential adverse consequences in the event of a breach (exactly the same as the NDB requirements, to be discussed shortly).

More information can be found in APP 11 here: www.oaic.gov.au/privacy/australian-privacy-principles/australian-privacy-principles-guidelines/chapter-11-app-11-security-of-personal-information.

Section 11.8 in the APP guidelines defines: "Reasonable steps should include, where relevant, taking steps and implementing strategies in relation to the following:

- governance, culture and training

- internal practices, procedures and systems

- ICT security

- access security

- third party providers (including cloud computing)

- data breaches

- physical security

- destruction and de-identification

- standards."

Additionally, noncompliance with APP 11 can result in significant fines for the organization. The Office of the Australian Information Commissioner (OAIC) has the power to issue infringement notices with fines of up to $52,200 for each breach of the APP.

So APP 11 is the main principles that directors will focus on when satisfying their obligations under the APP, but what about the other principles and how they relate to director obligations?

The 13 Australian Privacy Principles (APPs) translate into several key obligations for directors and boards. In terms of mapping the obligations to board responsibility, it encompasses two areas:

General Obligations

> **Privacy Policy and Oversight (APPs 1, 5, and 6):**
> The board should ensure a clear and up-to-date privacy policy exists, outlining data collection, use, and disclosure practices. They should oversee its implementation and adherence.
>
> **Risk Management (APP 11):** The board has a duty to manage privacy risks. This includes implementing appropriate security measures to protect personal information and regularly reviewing these measures.
>
> **Compliance Culture (All APPs):** Directors and the board should foster a culture of privacy compliance within the organization. This involves training staff and ensuring they understand their privacy obligations.

Specific Obligations by Principle

Anonymity (APP 2): The board should consider if anonymous interactions are feasible and encourage their use where possible.

Collection Practices (APP 3): Directors should ensure the organization only collects personal information necessary for its functions and does so lawfully and fairly.

Unsolicited Information (APP 4): The board needs to establish procedures for handling unsolicited personal information.

Direct Marketing (APP 7): The board should ensure individuals have clear opt-out options for receiving marketing messages.

Cross-Border Disclosure (APP 8): Directors must ensure overseas transfers of personal information comply with the APPs and consider the receiving country's privacy safeguards.

Access and Correction (APP 9): The board should ensure there are clear processes for individuals to access and correct their personal information held by the organization.

Data Quality (APP 10): Directors have a responsibility to ensure the accuracy, completeness, and currency of personal information the organization holds.

Data Identifiers (APP 12): The board should understand the regulations around data identifiers and ensure their use complies with the APPs.

Sensitive Information (APP 13): Directors should ensure the organization obtains consent before collecting sensitive information and has appropriate safeguards in place.

3.2 Real-World Example – Telstra APP Breach

Telstra found itself in hot water in 2023. The Office of the Australian Information Commissioner (OAIC) launched an investigation after it was revealed Telstra had been collecting customer location data for years, even when their phones were switched off. This blatant disregard for Australian Privacy Principle (APP) 3 – a collection of personal information – sparked outrage. Customers felt their privacy had been seriously invaded.

Matters worsened when a hacker infiltrated Telstra's systems, exploiting a vulnerability that had gone unnoticed due to lax cybersecurity practices. The breach exposed the very same location data Telstra had been improperly collecting. Millions of customer names, addresses, and, most alarmingly, their historical movements were compromised. The fallout was immense. Telstra faced a hefty fine from the OAIC for breaching privacy laws and a class-action lawsuit from customers whose data was exposed. The company's reputation was tarnished and public trust severely eroded. This incident served as a stark reminder for all Australian organizations that adhering to privacy principles and robust cybersecurity practices is not just a legal obligation but essential for maintaining customer trust.

3.3 Notifiable Data Breaches Scheme [13]

The Notifiable Data Breaches (NDB) scheme is in fact a section of the Privacy Act (Part IIIC) which requires organizations to notify individuals and the Office of the Australian Information Commissioner (OAIC) about eligible data breaches.

The scheme applies to any entities that have existing obligations under the Privacy Act to secure personal information and includes Australian Government agencies, businesses, and not-for-profit organizations that have an annual turnover of more than AU$3 million, as well as private sector health service providers, credit reporting bodies, credit providers, entities that trade in personal information and tax file number (TFN) recipients.

Realistically though, all organizations hold PII, or personally identifiable information, in one form or another, so in most circumstances, sub–$3 million organizations still need to comply with the NDB scheme.

What defines an eligible breach?

An eligible data breach is a data breach where:

- There is unauthorized access to or unauthorized disclosure of personal information, or a loss of personal information, that an entity holds.

- And that the information exposed is likely to result in serious harm to one or more individuals and that the entity has not been able to prevent the likely risk of serious harm with remedial action.

What constitutes serious harm?

Serious harm to an individual may include serious physical, psychological, emotional, financial, or reputational harm and should be benchmarked against the type of information exposed, the circumstances associated with the breach, the number of affected individuals, how long the information has been exposed, whether the data was anonymized or can be tied back to the individual, and what parties may have gained access to the data.

An organization has a 30-day maximum limit to report the breach to the OAIC, complete the assessment, perform remedial actions, and contact the affected individuals.

The OAIC understands that breaches happen, but if the OAIC chooses to investigate, they will be seeking assurances that you have done your due diligence as an organization (and a board) to protect the data that has been exposed. Failure to notify the OAIC of a data breach within the required timeframe or adequately responding to a breach can result in significant fines. The OAIC can impose fines of up to and over $2 million for a single breach. In particular, they will be looking at practices, procedures, response plans, and systems in place for the organization, to ensure that they comply with their information security obligations under APP 11, enabling suspected breaches to be promptly identified, assessed, and reported to relevant personnel.

While the Australian Privacy Principles (APP 11) and the Notifiable Data Breaches (NDB) scheme apply broadly, certain industries have additional cybersecurity obligations. Directors in particular industries should be aware of additional obligations that are industry specific, such as follows:

> **Healthcare:** Healthcare organizations are entrusted with sensitive patient data. The Australian Digital Health Agency (DHAA) outlines cybersecurity requirements for healthcare providers, including mandatory data breach reporting and adherence to the Australian Cyber Security Measures for Health Services (ACSMS) framework. More information can be found here: www.digitalhealth.gov.au/healthcare-providers/cyber-security.

> **Energy:** The Australian Energy Market Operator (AEMO) requires energy sector participants to implement cybersecurity measures to protect critical infrastructure. This includes complying with the Energy Sector Cyber Security Framework (ESCSF). More information can be found here: https://aemo.com.au/en/initiatives/major-programs/cyber-security/aescsf-framework-and-resources.

Understanding industry-specific regulations is crucial for directors to ensure their organization meets all cybersecurity compliance requirements. For a comprehensive understanding, consult with legal counsel or cybersecurity professionals specializing in your industry.

It is important to note that the Australian Government is currently considering reforms to the Notifiable Data Breach Scheme (NDBS) that may tighten obligations for organizations. These reforms are expected to focus on enhancing data security requirements and tightening reporting timeframes.

3.3.1 A Note on PHI vs. PII in the Context of the NDBS

Protected health information (PHI) is another area that can be confusing for directors to understand how this applies in the context of the NDBS. PHI is a specific subset of personally identifiable information (PII). PII refers to any data that can be used to identify an individual, such as name, address, or tax file number. PHI, on the other hand, focuses exclusively on health information that can be linked to a person. This includes medical records, diagnoses, treatment details, and insurance information. The key distinction lies in the context of the data. PII on its own might not reveal health details, but when combined with PHI, it becomes identifiable health information.

The Notifiable Data Breach Scheme (NDBS) mandates organizations to report data breaches involving personal information to the OAIC. This includes OHI (other health identifiers), which are any unique identifiers used in the healthcare sector to identify individuals. Examples of OHI include Medicare numbers, private health insurance identifiers, and universal patient identifiers. If a data breach compromises any of these identifiers along with other health information, it falls under the NDBS reporting requirements. Essentially, the NDBS acts as a safeguard to ensure timely notification of potential healthcare privacy breaches.

3.4 The Corporations Act 2001 (Cth) [14]

The Corporations Act 2001 (Cth) plays a crucial role in director responsibilities related to cybersecurity. Under Section 180, directors have a duty of care and must ensure due diligence to protect the organization's assets. This includes ensuring that the organization's cybersecurity strategy adequately safeguards its key data and systems.

Failure to implement adequate cybersecurity measures could be seen as a breach of directors' duties under the Corporations Act, potentially leading to legal repercussions.

You can find more information about directors' duties on the ASIC website: `https://asic.gov.au/for-business/small-business/starting-a-small-business-company/small-business-company-directors/`.

Directors of entities that hold an Australian Financial Services License (AFSL) must comply with the general and specific obligations under the Corporations Act.

3.5 Real-World Example – Corporation Act Failure

In 2020, the Australian Securities and Investments Commission (ASIC) took action against RI Advice, a financial services licensee. The issue stemmed from a cyberattack in 2019 that compromised the personal information of over 17,000 clients. ASIC found that RI Advice had failed to meet its obligations under the Corporations Act, specifically section 912A, which mandates adequate cybersecurity measures. The investigation revealed RI Advice lacked proper data security protocols, had outdated software, and hadn't conducted thorough staff training on cyber risks.

These shortcomings directly contributed to the successful cyberattack. ASIC emphasized that directors have a duty to exercise reasonable care and diligence in managing cyber risks. As a consequence, RI Advice faced a significant fine from ASIC, which was a stark reminder for Australian organizations to prioritize cybersecurity and data protection.

3.6 International Obligations for Cybersecurity and PII for Australian Organizations Operating Globally

If your organization doesn't operate globally or deal with other regions, you can skip this section. For those of you who do transact, partner with, or operate in other countries, let's explore the key international obligations Australian businesses encounter when handling personal data, focusing on prominent regulations like the European Union's General Data Protection Regulation (GDPR) and others with extraterritorial reach.

The GDPR and Its Applicability to Australian Organizations
The General Data Protection Regulation (GDPR), implemented in the European Union (EU) in 2018, is one of the most stringent data privacy regulations globally. The GDPR applies to any organization processing the personal data of individuals residing in the EU, regardless of the organization's physical location. This extraterritorial reach can have significant implications for Australian businesses with EU-based customers or operations that process EU citizen data.

Key Requirements of the GDPR for Australian Organizations
GDPR encompasses a number of requirements that directors and board members should be aware of; these include

Lawful Basis for Processing: The GDPR mandates a lawful basis for processing personal data, such as consent, contractual necessity, or legitimate interests. Australian organizations must identify the appropriate legal basis for processing EU citizen data.

Data Subject Rights: The GDPR grants EU residents various rights regarding their personal data, including the right to access, rectify, erase, and restrict processing. Australian organizations must implement procedures to fulfill these rights for EU data subjects.

Data Transfer Adequacy: Transferring personal data outside the EU requires ensuring an adequate level of protection in the receiving country. The Australian Privacy Act may not always be considered adequate, so Australian businesses may need to rely on additional mechanisms like Standard Contractual Clauses (SCCs) to transfer data lawfully.

Appointment of a Representative: If an Australian organization offers goods or services to EU residents or monitors their behavior, they may need to appoint a representative within the EU to act as a point of contact for data subjects and supervisory authorities.

Data Breach Notification: The GDPR requires notification of data breaches to affected individuals and potentially the relevant supervisory authority within specific timeframes. Australian organizations must comply with these notification requirements if they experience breaches involving EU citizen data.

US Requirements Applicable to Australian Organizations

Australian organizations transferring personal data to the United States need to comply with the Australian Privacy Act 1988 (Cth) and specifically the Australian Privacy Principles (APPs). The Privacy Act allows transfers of personal data overseas, but organizations must take "reasonable steps" to ensure the recipient in the United States protects the information in a way that is substantially similar to the APPs.

The only real requirements from a general data protection level are the California Consumer Privacy Act (CCPA) and California Privacy Rights Act (CPRA). These California laws grant similar data subject rights to California residents. Australian organizations doing business in California may need to comply with these regulations.

You may also be familiar with what used to be called the US Privacy Shield (invalidated August 2020), which was previously a mechanism for data transfers between the United States and EU. Australian organizations transferring personal data to the United States should rely on alternative mechanisms like SCCs.

Standard Contractual Clauses (SCCs) are preapproved contracts developed by the European Commission that can be used by organizations to transfer data to/from the EU and the United States. While not directly endorsed by Australian legislation, SCCs are a recognized way to meet the "reasonable steps" requirement.

There are also industry-specific requirements that may come into play for your organization, depending on the data you are handling and the operating functions of the organization, such as:

> **Healthcare:** The Health Insurance Portability and Accountability Act (HIPAA) applies to Australian organizations only if they handle the protected health information of US citizens, requiring them to comply with HIPAA's data privacy and security standards.

Financial Services: The Gramm–Leach–Bliley Act (GLBA) in the United States (and the General Data Protection Regulation for Banking (GDPR-Banking) in Europe) regulates data handling practices in the financial services industry.

Telecommunications: Regulations like the Federal Communications Commission (FCC) rules in the United States and the Directive on Privacy and Electronic Communications (ePrivacy Directive) in Europe govern data collection and usage practices by telecommunication companies.

APAC Requirements Applicable to Australian Organizations

There is only one data handling principle, which is called the APEC Cross-Border Privacy Rules (CBPR), and it is not legally binding and provides more of a guidance for Australian businesses operating in APEC economies. It also promotes data privacy cooperation within the Asia-Pacific Economic Cooperation (APEC) region.

Understanding the data your organization collects and where it resides is crucial. Directors can take proactive steps by initiating data mapping exercises to identify the flow of personal information, particularly for EU residents and Californian consumers. Additionally, appointing a data protection officer (DPO) specifically for the EU can be a valuable strategy. This dedicated resource can serve as a point of contact for regulators and individuals, ensuring GDPR compliance is embedded within your organization's practices. For US operations, directors should also consider the applicability of CCPA and CPRA, potentially requiring the development of similar mechanisms for handling data subject requests.

3.7 Key Questions for Your Organization

- Are we familiar with the Australian Privacy Principles (APP 11) and our obligations to protect personal information?

- Have we taken reasonable steps to protect the personal information (PII) we hold, considering factors like the sensitivity of the information and potential consequences of a breach?

- Do we regularly review and update our data handling practices to ensure compliance with APP 11?

- Have we implemented appropriate security measures (e.g., access controls, encryption) to safeguard PII?

- Do we have a process for securely destroying or de-identifying personal information when it is no longer needed?

- Do we understand our obligations under the NDB scheme, including the criteria for an eligible data breach?

- Have we established a process for assessing and reporting eligible data breaches to the OAIC and affected individuals within 30 days?

- Do we have a plan in place to mitigate the risk of serious harm to individuals in the event of a data breach?

- Are we aware of our directors' duties under the Corporations Act, particularly regarding the duty of care and diligence in protecting the organization's assets, including data?

- Have we implemented adequate cybersecurity measures to fulfill these duties and protect the organization from potential legal repercussions?

- If our organization operates globally or handles the personal data of individuals in other regions (e.g., EU, the United States), do we understand and comply with relevant international data protection regulations like the GDPR, CCPA, or CPRA?

- Have we implemented appropriate mechanisms (e.g., Standard Contractual Clauses) for lawful data transfers across borders?

3.8 Key Takeaways

- Directors should demonstrate proactive leadership by fostering a strong cybersecurity culture that goes beyond mere compliance.

- The Australian Privacy Principles (APP 11) requires reasonable steps to secure personal information (PII) and manage data breaches.

- The Notifiable Data Breaches (NDB) scheme requires reporting data breaches to regulators and affected individuals within 30 days.

- There can be significant fines for organizations failing to meet APP 11 or NDB requirements.

- Directors should be aware of any international data handling requirements and cybersecurity requirements if they are operating outside of the ANZ region, such as GDPR.

- There are potential legal repercussions for directors for breaching their duty of care under the Corporations Act.

References

[12]   www.oaic.gov.au/privacy/australian-privacy-principles/ australian-privacy-principles-guidelines/chapter-11- app-11-security-of-personal-information

[13]   www.oaic.gov.au/privacy/notifiable-data-breaches/ about-the-notifiable-data-breaches-scheme

[14]   www.legislation.gov.au/C2004A00818/latest/text

CHAPTER 4

Common Cyber Governance Principles and Standards

There are a number of cyber governance principles and standards that are adopted or adhered to by organizations in Australia (and enforced/managed by boards).

These include:

- ASD/ACSC Cyber Security Guidelines

- AICD Cyber Security Governance Principles

- ASIC cybersecurity requirements

- APRA Prudential Standard – CPS 231/234

- Critical Infrastructure Risk Management Program

- SOCI Act 2018 for Telecommunications

- CISC (Cyber and Infrastructure Security Centre) guidance

By far the most common standards/governance principles adhered to by boards and organizations are AICD, ASIC, and APRA.

© The Editor(s) (if applicable) and The Author(s),
under exclusive license to APress Media, LLC, part of Springer Nature 2024
D. Weis, *Boardroom Cybersecurity*, https://doi.org/10.1007/979-8-8688-0785-5_4

4.1 AICD Cyber Security Governance Principles

The AICD Cyber Security Governance Principles provide a framework for Australian organizations to improve their cyber resilience. In summary, the key principles are:

1. **Set Clear Roles and Responsibilities:**

   Clearly define who is responsible for cybersecurity at all levels of the organization, including board oversight, management accountability, and employee awareness.

2. **Develop, Implement, and Evaluate a Comprehensive Cyber Strategy:**

   Create a proactive cybersecurity strategy aligned with the organization's risk profile and business objectives. This strategy should address areas such as data protection, incident response, and employee training.

3. **Embed Cybersecurity in Existing Risk Management Practices:**

   Integrate cybersecurity risk assessment and mitigation strategies into existing risk management frameworks.

4. **Promote a Culture of Cyber Resilience:**

   Foster a culture of awareness where cybersecurity is everyone's responsibility. This involves regular employee training, awareness campaigns, and open communication about cyber threats.

5. **Plan for a Significant Cybersecurity Incident:**

   Develop a robust incident response plan to effectively identify, contain, and recover from a cyberattack.

These principles are designed to help organizations of all sizes improve their cybersecurity posture and better manage cyber risks in today's digital age.

4.2 ASIC Cybersecurity Requirements

The ASIC cybersecurity requirements focus on ensuring a minimum standard of cybersecurity practices for organizations they regulate, primarily in the financial sector (listed companies, financial institutions, and credit licensees). In summary, the key aspects are:

Governance and Oversight:

Boards and senior management must have a clear understanding of cybersecurity risks and implement appropriate governance frameworks.

Risk Management:

Organizations need to identify, assess, and manage cybersecurity risks as part of their overall risk management strategy.

Incident Reporting:

Specific requirements exist for reporting cybersecurity incidents to ASIC depending on the nature and severity of the incident.

Protecting Customer Data:

Robust measures are required to safeguard customer data, including data encryption, access controls, and data breach notification procedures.

Control Environment:

ASIC requirements may outline specific controls or security measures that organizations need to implement to protect their systems and data.

Continuous Improvement:

Organizations are expected to continuously improve their cybersecurity posture through regular monitoring, vulnerability management, and staff training.

It's important to note that these are general points, and the specific requirements can vary. You can find relevant resources on the ASIC website here: https://asic.gov.au/regulatory-resources/corporate-governance/cyber-resilience/.

4.3 APRA Prudential Standard – CPS 231/234

The APRA prudential has two standards focused on cybersecurity: CPS 234 Information Security and CPS 231 Cyber Security Incident Reporting.

Key Requirements – CPS 231 (Cyber Security Incident Reporting):

Incident Reporting: Entities must report significant cybersecurity incidents to APRA within specific timeframes, detailing the nature, impact, response, and lessons learned.

Governance and Oversight: Emphasizes board and senior management oversight of cybersecurity risks and clear roles/responsibilities.

Risk Management: Requires a comprehensive cybersecurity risk management framework to identify, assess, and manage cyber threats.

Cybersecurity Capability and Controls: While not mandating specific controls, it emphasizes appropriate measures to protect data and systems (encryption, access controls, etc.).

Business Continuity and Recovery: Documented plans for responding to and recovering from cybersecurity incidents.

Employee Awareness and Training: Importance of ongoing staff training on cybersecurity risks and best practices.

Key Requirements – CPS 234 (Information Security):

Information Security Capability: Maintain a capability to protect information assets and ensure business continuity in case of an attack.

Risk Management: Ongoing identification, assessment, and management of information security risks, adapting to the evolving threat landscape.

Information Security Policy Framework: Develop and maintain a comprehensive framework with policies, procedures, and controls to safeguard information.

Data Protection: Emphasizes protecting sensitive data (customer data, financial information, intellectual property) through encryption, access controls, and data breach notification procedures.

Business Continuity and Recovery: Similar to CPS 231, requires documented plans for recovery from security incidents with minimal disruption.

Accountability and Oversight: Board and senior management oversight of information security with clear roles and responsibilities within the organization.

How They Work Together

CPS 231 and CPS 234 are complementary standards. CPS 231 focuses on the specific reporting requirements for cybersecurity incidents, and CPS 234 establishes a broader information security framework, encompassing cyber threats and other risks to sensitive information.

Together, they ensure APRA-regulated entities have a robust information security program to manage cyber risks effectively, protect valuable information assets, and report significant incidents to the regulator.

4.4 ASIC Cybersecurity Requirements vs. AICD Cyber Security Governance Principles vs. APRA Requirements for Cybersecurity

A common question I often receive from boards is what the difference is between ASIC, APRA, and AICD cybersecurity guidance and requirements.

The ASIC requirements for cybersecurity and the AICD Cyber Security Governance Principles serve different purposes but can be seen as complementary approaches to cybersecurity for organizations in Australia. Similarly, APRA and ASIC requirements are very similar. Here's a breakdown of the key differences:

ASIC Requirements:

- **Focus:** Regulatory requirements.

- **Enforcement:** Legally enforceable by ASIC.

- **Specificity:** May outline specific controls or reporting obligations.

- **Target Audience:** Primarily applies to entities regulated by ASIC, such as listed companies, financial institutions, and credit licensees.

- **Overall Approach:** Prescriptive, outlining minimum compliance standards.

APRA Requirements:

- **Focus:** Prudential regulation for entities in the banking, superannuation, and insurance sectors.

- **Enforcement:** Legally enforceable through prudential standards (CPS 231) and guidance.

- **Specificity:** Similar to ASIC, outlines specific controls and reporting requirements within CPS 231 (Cyber Security Incident Reporting).

- **Target Audience:** Banks, credit unions, insurers, and superannuation entities.

- **Overall Approach:** Prescriptive, requiring entities to implement specific controls and report incidents.

AICD Cyber Security Governance Principles:

- **Focus:** Best practices and guidance.

- **Enforcement:** Not legally enforceable but promotes good corporate governance.

47

- **Specificity:** Provides a framework of principles rather than specific controls.

- **Target Audience:** Broader audience, applicable to all Australian organizations regardless of industry or size.

- **Overall Approach:** Principles-based, encouraging a proactive approach to cybersecurity.

Summarizing the differences:

Feature	ASIC Requirements	AICD Cyber Security Governance Principles	APRA Requirements
Focus	Regulatory Compliance (financial sector)	Best practices and guidance (Broader)	Prudential regulation (banking, superannuation, insurance)
Enforcement	Legally enforceable	Not legally enforceable	Legally enforceable
Specificity	May outline specific controls	Provides a framework of principles	Specific controls outlined in CPS 231
Target Audience	ASIC-regulated entities	All Australian organizations	Banks, credit unions, insurers, and superannuation entities
Overall Approach	Prescriptive (minimum standards)	Principles-based (proactive approach)	Prescriptive (specific controls)

4.5 How They Work Together

ASIC requirements act as a baseline for cybersecurity compliance, ensuring a certain level of protection for consumers and financial systems. The AICD principles then build upon this foundation by encouraging organizations to adopt a more proactive and holistic approach to cybersecurity governance.

These three frameworks create a layered approach to cybersecurity for Australian organizations, especially those in the financial sector. Some ways they can work together in practice:

- APRA sets the baseline for regulated entities. Their specific requirements outlined in CPS 231 ensure a strong foundation for cybersecurity within the banking, superannuation, and insurance industries.

- ASIC builds upon APRA requirements for some entities. Organizations that fall under both APRA and ASIC regulations will need to comply with both sets of requirements. ASIC requirements can inform the implementation of AICD principles. For example, an ASIC requirement for reporting cybersecurity incidents can be addressed through an AICD principle that focuses on incident response planning and communication.

- AICD principles can be applied by all organizations and can help organizations exceed the minimum compliance standards set by ASIC and APRA. Regardless of industry or size, all Australian organizations can benefit from adopting a framework based on the AICD principles to strengthen their cybersecurity posture beyond the minimum regulatory requirements. By adopting a robust cybersecurity framework aligned with the AICD principles, organizations can demonstrate strong corporate governance and potentially mitigate future risks beyond what the regulations might mandate.

Do Any of These Three Requirements Conflict?

There isn't any direct conflict, but additional consideration is required:

Specificity vs. Applicability: While ASIC and APRA provide more specific controls, these controls might not be directly applicable to all organizations under the AICD framework. Organizations should adapt the AICD principles to their specific needs and context.

Compliance vs. Proactive Approach: The focus on compliance with ASIC and APRA requirements shouldn't overshadow the importance of a proactive cybersecurity strategy based on the AICD principles. Organizations can use AICD principles to go beyond minimum compliance and build a more robust cyber defense.

Overall, these frameworks work together to improve cybersecurity. Understanding the differences and how they complement each other helps organizations comply with regulations while also adopting a proactive and holistic approach to cybersecurity governance.

4.6 Real-World Example – Sunshine Coast Health Network

A slightly older example but a good one when it comes to missing security governance, principles, and standards is the Sunshine Coast Health Network (SCH). This incident highlights the devastating consequences of neglecting security governance principles and standards.

Back in 2016, a ransomware attack crippled their IT systems, throwing critical patient care services into disarray.

At the heart of the problem was SCH's lack of a robust cybersecurity program. The organization lacked a dedicated security team, and security responsibilities were scattered across various departments with no clear ownership. This fragmented approach meant there were no formal security policies or standards to guide their practices. The absence of a centralized security strategy and defined security measures left their defenses wide open for exploitation.

The attackers capitalized on this vulnerability by exploiting a known gap in outdated software used by SCH. A defined patching process would have addressed this vulnerability, but unfortunately, such a process was absent. This oversight allowed the attackers to gain a foothold in the network. Once inside, they deployed ransomware, and patient records, medical images, and administrative systems all fell victim to this encryption.

The attack sent shockwaves through SCH. Doctors and nurses struggled to access vital patient records, hindering diagnoses and treatment. Appointments were canceled, and critical operations had to be postponed. The hospital was forced to revert to pen-and-paper records, significantly impacting efficiency and jeopardizing patient care.

Recovering from the attack was a long and arduous battle. While SCH had backups, they were neither complete nor up-to-date, resulting in data loss. The financial cost of recovery was substantial, encompassing the ransom payment, data restoration expenses, and the lost productivity due to the downtime.

The SCH incident serves as a chilling reminder of the importance of strong security governance. If we sit back and analyze their shortcomings that led to the breach, we observe the following:

> **Lack of Security Leadership:** The absence of a dedicated security team and unclear ownership of security responsibilities resulted in a fragmented approach to cybersecurity.

51

No Security Policies or Standards: Without a defined road map in the form of security policies and standards, SCH lacked direction in securing their systems and data.

Patch Management Failures: The lack of a rigorous patch management process left outdated software vulnerable to known exploits, creating an entry point for attackers.

Inadequate Backups: Incomplete or outdated backups significantly hampered data recovery efforts and potentially led to greater data loss.

Following the attack, SCH undertook a major security overhaul. They established a dedicated security team, developed security policies and standards, implemented a proper patch management process, and improved their backup protocols. Additionally, they invested in employee security awareness training to further strengthen their defenses.

The SCH incident is a reminder of the critical need for continuous vigilance and adaptation in cybersecurity. Organizations must regularly assess their security posture, identify and address vulnerabilities, and stay updated on the ever-evolving cyber threat landscape. By prioritizing security governance, organizations like SCH can significantly reduce the risk of cyberattacks and safeguard their critical data.

Interestingly, in 2021, the exact same attack and scenario played out for Eastern Health (one of the largest groups of hospitals in Victoria). The same shortcomings were identified.

4.7 Key Questions for Your Organization

- Do we have a clear understanding of the cybersecurity risks specific to our industry and organization?

- What governance and standards requirements are applicable to our organization and industry, such as the ASIC cybersecurity requirements or APRA Prudential Standard CPS 231/234?

- Have we adopted a recognized cyber governance framework or standard, such as the AICD Cyber Security Governance Principles, ASIC cybersecurity requirements, or APRA Prudential Standard CPS 231/234?

- Do we understand the key principles and requirements of our chosen framework or standard and how they apply to our organization?

- Are we regularly assessing our organization's cyber resilience against the chosen framework or standard?

- Do we have a process for addressing any gaps or weaknesses identified in these assessments?

- Have we clearly defined roles and responsibilities for cybersecurity at all levels of the organization, including the board, management, and employees?

- Do we have a comprehensive cyber strategy in place that aligns with our risk profile and business objectives? This should include incident response planning, data protection measures, and employee training.

- Are we regularly evaluating and updating our cyber strategy to address evolving threats and technologies?

- Are we embedding cybersecurity into our existing risk management practices?

- Are we promoting a culture of cyber resilience throughout the organization, including regular employee training and awareness campaigns?

- Do we have a robust incident response plan in place to effectively manage a significant cybersecurity incident?

4.8 Key Takeaways

- Multiple frameworks guide Australian organizations in building, maintaining, and reviewing cyber resilience.

- Key options include AICD principles, ASIC requirements, and APRA standards (CPS 231/234).

  - **AICD:** Best practices and principles (broader audience and applicability, not enforced).

  - **ASIC:** Legally enforceable regulations for financial institutions.

  - **APRA:** Enforced standards for banking, superannuation, and insurance (CPS 231/234).

- Meeting regulations shouldn't replace a proactive cyber strategy.

CHAPTER 5

Cybersecurity Frameworks

Now let's talk frameworks. It's important for directors to understand how cybersecurity frameworks differ from governance principles. There are two main differences between a framework and a governance principle; these are

1. **Specificity:** Frameworks are more specific than governance principles. They provide concrete steps and recommendations for implementing security measures.

2. **Focus:** Frameworks focus on the technical aspects of cybersecurity, while governance principles are broader, encompassing leadership oversight, risk management, and cultural aspects of security.

So think of it this way:

Cybersecurity Frameworks: Are a road map outlining the "what" and "how" of securing your organization (specific actions and controls).

Governance Principles: Are a set of guiding values outlining the "why" and overall approach to cybersecurity (leadership commitment and risk management strategy).

© The Editor(s) (if applicable) and The Author(s),
under exclusive license to APress Media, LLC, part of Springer Nature 2024
D. Weis, *Boardroom Cybersecurity*, https://doi.org/10.1007/979-8-8688-0785-5_5

They both play a key role and complement each other, with both essential for a well-rounded cybersecurity strategy. Frameworks provide the technical road map for securing your organization, while governance principles set the overall direction and ensure leadership commitment to cyber risk management.

There are several reasons why an organization would adopt a cybersecurity framework:

Improved Security Posture: Frameworks provide a structured approach to identifying and addressing cybersecurity risks. They outline best practices for areas such as access control, data protection, incident response, and employee training. By following a framework, organizations can systematically improve their overall security posture and better mitigate potential vulnerabilities.

Compliance with Regulations: Many regulations, particularly in financial services and healthcare, incorporate elements of established cybersecurity frameworks. Implementing a framework can help organizations demonstrate compliance with these regulations and avoid potential penalties.

Risk Management: Frameworks help organizations identify, assess, and prioritize cybersecurity risks. This enables effective allocation of resources and focus on the most critical areas to protect.

Standardization and Consistency: Frameworks provide a common language and set of best practices across the organization. This helps ensure all departments and employees are working toward the same cybersecurity goals and reduces the risk of inconsistencies or gaps in security measures.

Improved Communication and Collaboration:
Frameworks can facilitate communication and
collaboration between different teams within an
organization, such as IT, security, and business units.
This fosters a more unified approach to cybersecurity.

Benchmarking and Improvement: Frameworks
often include metrics and benchmarks that allow
organizations to measure their cybersecurity maturity
and track progress over time. This enables them to
identify areas for improvement and continuously
enhance their security posture.

There are a number of common cybersecurity frameworks adopted in
Australia, including the following:

5.1 ACSC Essential Eight

The Essential Eight [15] was developed by the Australian Cyber Security
Centre (ACSC) in June 2017 to serve as a baseline security standard for
Australian businesses, to make it harder for adversaries to compromise
systems, and to mitigate cybersecurity threats and data breaches. This
framework is also recommended by the Australian Signals Directorate
(ASD) for all Australian organizations.

The Essential Eight (also known as the ASD Essential Eight or E8) is
comprised of eight basic mitigation strategies, or security controls, that are
divided across three primary objectives.

The mitigation strategies encompass

Prevention:

- Application control

- Patch applications

- Restrict Microsoft Office macros

- User application hardening

Limit Attack Impact:

- Restrict administrative privileges

- Patch operating systems

- Multi-factor authentication

Data Availability:

- Regular backups

The Essential Eight standard also measures maturity levels ranging from zero to three [16]:

- **Maturity Level One:** Partially aligned with the mitigation strategy objectives

- **Maturity Level Two:** Mostly aligned with the mitigation strategy objectives

- **Maturity Level Three:** Fully aligned with the mitigation strategy objectives

The Essential Eight is one of the most adopted frameworks adopted by Australian organizations as it involves a smaller or more manageable baseline of activities and actions but with the highest return on investment in terms of reducing an organization's risk profile.

5.2 NIST Cybersecurity Framework

The NIST Cybersecurity Framework (CSF) [17] is a voluntary, non-prescriptive framework that helps organizations of all sizes manage and reduce their cybersecurity risks. Its key aspects center around improving an organization's overall cybersecurity posture and identifying, protecting, detecting, responding to, and recovering from cyber threats.

The framework is built around five core functions:

1. **Identify:** Identify critical assets, systems, and data. Understand the cyber threats your organization faces.

2. **Protect:** Develop and implement safeguards to ensure the availability, integrity, and confidentiality of your assets.

3. **Detect:** Implement activities to identify and report security incidents promptly.

4. **Respond:** Take appropriate actions to contain, eradicate, and recover from a security incident.

5. **Recover:** Develop and implement plans to restore essential functions after a security incident.

The NIST CSF encompasses a number of benefits including

- **Flexibility:** The framework is adaptable to any organization's size, industry, and risk profile.

- **Cost-effectiveness:** It focuses on prioritized actions based on risk, allowing organizations to optimize their cybersecurity investments.

- **Improved Communication:** It provides a common language for discussing cybersecurity within the organization.

- **Alignment with Regulations:** The framework can help organizations comply with various cybersecurity regulations and standards.

The NIST CSF doesn't dictate specific controls but rather provides a framework for organizations to develop their own cybersecurity program based on their needs. It includes resources and recommendations for implementing each of the core functions.

Another benefit is that organizations can leverage the framework partially or entirely based on their specific context.

5.3 CIS Controls

The CIS Controls [18], formally known as the CIS Critical Security Controls (CIS CSC), are a prioritized set of best practices intended to mitigate the most prevalent cyber threats and vulnerabilities. They are designed to be a foundational element of any organization's cybersecurity strategy, providing a baseline for effective cybersecurity.

It consists of 18 controls, split into six pillars, encompassing

- **Inventory and Control of Assets:** Identify and manage all hardware, software, and data

- **Boundary Defense:** Protect the network perimeter

- **Data Protection:** Secure sensitive information

- **Account Management:** Control access to systems and data

- **Maintenance, Monitoring, and Analysis:** Detect and respond to threats

- **Continuous Improvement:** Regularly assess and improve security posture

Implementing the CIS Controls can provide a number of benefits and significantly reduce the likelihood of successful cyberattacks by addressing common vulnerabilities. This includes

- **Improved Compliance:** The CIS Controls align with many cybersecurity regulations and standards, making them a valuable tool for demonstrating compliance.

- **Cost-effectiveness:** Focusing on these prioritized controls allows organizations to optimize their cybersecurity investments.

- **Flexibility:** The CIS Controls can be adapted to organizations of all sizes and industries.

Similar to the National Institute of Standards and Technology (NIST), the CIS Controls are not a one-size-fits-all solution. Organizations can choose to implement all the controls or prioritize those that address their most significant risks.

I'll also note that the CIS Controls are a starting point, and organizations should build upon them with additional security measures based on their specific risk profile and industry requirements (same with any framework really).

5.4 So, What Are the Differences Between These Three Frameworks, and Why Would I Choose One Over Another?

All of these frameworks have three different focus areas:

ACSC Essential Eight: Prevention-focused on mitigating the most prevalent cyber threats in Australia. This framework is predominantly technology centric.

NIST CSF: Holistic approach to managing cybersecurity risk across five core functions: identify, protect, detect, respond, and recover. This framework covers people, processes, technology, and governance (so a more holistic approach).

CIS Controls: Prioritized set of best practices to address the most common cyber vulnerabilities. This framework is more focused on individual controls within the security realms.

All frameworks can be adopted by various organizations; however, the ACSC E8 is targeted toward Australian organizations, particularly those in critical infrastructure sectors, whereas the NIST CSF is more broadly applicable to organizations of all sizes and industries, globally.

The CIS Controls are an industry-agnostic framework and can be adapted to various organizations; however, the NIST CSF can be applied more broadly to all organizations than the CISC, which is why we tend to see more prevalence of NIST.

If we examine the level of detail between these three frameworks, the ACSC E8 provides high-level recommendations, outlining what needs to be achieved but not always how.

The NIST CSF provides a framework with recommendations and resources but doesn't dictate specific controls. However, the CIS Controls are more specific than the others, offering a set of actionable control activities.

Adopting any security framework is a good idea, and all three frameworks aim to improve an organization's overall cybersecurity posture.

They all address critical security areas like access control, data protection, and incident response, and all three can be used to demonstrate compliance with various cybersecurity regulations.

I'll also add that organisations should seek guidance from cybersecurity professionals when selecting and implementing a framework. This can be particularly helpful for directors and boards without a technical background.

To help build understanding, I'll explain these three in an analogy to illustrate the differences. Imagine building a house...

ACSC Essential Eight: The building code – specifies essential elements for a secure structure.

NIST CSF: The construction manual – provides a road map for building a secure house but allows flexibility in materials and methods.

CIS Controls: A list of best practices for building a secure house – recommends specific actions like strong locks and fire alarms.

In summary:

- The ACSC Essential Eight provides a starting point for Australian organizations, focusing on essential actions to prevent common cyber threats.

- The NIST CSF offers a comprehensive framework for managing cybersecurity risk, adaptable to any organization's needs.

- The CIS Controls provide a prioritized set of best practices to address foundational security vulnerabilities.

It should also be noted that organizations don't have to pick one framework; they can leverage all three frameworks, for example, use the ACSC Essential Eight as a baseline, implement the NIST CSF to develop a comprehensive cybersecurity program, and then use the CIS Controls to address specific security weaknesses and improve the organizations' overall security posture.

In terms of why an organization would choose one over another, it really comes down to the organization's current cyber maturity, investment, and resources, as well as what framework is best aligned to their industry and business objectives:

Simple, Quick Improvements That Focus on Prevention and Basic Hygiene: Choose the ACSC E8, as it's a good starting point to improve basic security posture.

Need a Comprehensive and Adaptable Framework:
NIST CSF is ideal for building a holistic cybersecurity
program with defined processes for all aspects of
security.

Need Detailed Controls and Best Practices: Choose
CIS Controls (often used alongside NIST CSF). The CIS
Controls complement NIST CSF or other frameworks by
providing specific best practices for implementation.

Remember, the best choice often involves a combination of these
frameworks depending on your organization's specific needs and
resources.

These three frameworks are the predominant security frameworks that
I typically encounter across all organizations. Some other lesser-known
frameworks include the following.

5.5 Cloud Controls Matrix (CCM)

The Cloud Control Matrix (CCM)[19], developed by the Cloud Security
Alliance (CSA), is a cybersecurity control framework specifically designed
for cloud computing environments. It offers a comprehensive and
systematic approach to assessing the security of cloud implementations.
It is organized around 17 domains, encompassing 197 control objectives
that outline specific security goals. The CCM also provides the ability to
assess security risks and responsibilities within the cloud supply chain and
provides guidance on which security controls should be implemented by
which cloud service providers (CSPs) and cloud service customers (CSCs)).

Businesses using cloud services typically leverage this framework
to assess cloud provider security and their own responsibilities. Cloud
providers often use the CCM to showcase their security posture.

Its features include

Shared Responsibility Model: Clearly defines the attribution of security responsibilities between CSPs and CSCs, fostering a collaborative approach to cloud security.

Systematic Assessment: Provides a structured method for evaluating the security posture of a cloud service based on industry-accepted control objectives.

Alignment with Standards: Maps to other security standards and regulations, allowing organizations to demonstrate compliance more easily.

Flexibility: Can be adapted to different cloud service models (IaaS, PaaS, SaaS) and the specific needs of an organization.

The CCM is more of a guidance document, and specific control implementations might vary depending on the chosen cloud service provider's offerings.

5.6 Australian Energy Sector Cyber Security Framework (AESCSF)

The Australian Energy Sector Cyber Security Framework (AESCSF)[20] is a tool designed to improve the cybersecurity posture of Australia's electricity, gas, and liquid fuels sectors.

Developed through collaboration between industry, government, and stakeholders, the AESCSF reflects the combined expertise of the energy sector. It provides a structured approach for energy organizations to

Assess Their Current Cybersecurity Maturity: The framework helps organizations evaluate their existing cybersecurity capabilities and identify areas for improvement.

Develop and Implement a Cybersecurity Improvement Plan: Based on the assessment, organizations can prioritize actions to strengthen their cybersecurity defenses.

Maintain a Strong Cybersecurity Posture: The AESCSF encourages ongoing monitoring, risk management, and adaptation to keep pace with the evolving cyber threat landscape.

The AESCSF leverages established cybersecurity frameworks like the NIST Cybersecurity Framework (CSF) and incorporates Australian-specific control references. It is very much focused on critical infrastructure and is tailored to the unique needs and risks of the energy sector, considering the critical nature of energy infrastructure.

Its benefits include:

Improved Cybersecurity: By following the framework, energy organizations can significantly enhance their cybersecurity posture and reduce the risk of cyberattacks.

Enhanced Resilience: A strong cybersecurity posture makes energy organizations more resilient to cyber threats, ensuring the continued reliable operation of critical infrastructure.

Regulatory Compliance: The AESCSF helps organizations comply with relevant cybersecurity regulations and standards within Australia.

Overall, the AESCSF serves as a valuable resource for the Australian energy sector, empowering organizations to build robust cybersecurity defenses and protect their critical infrastructure from cyber threats.

5.7 Control Objectives for Information Technology (COBIT)

COBIT [21], which stands for Control Objectives for Information Technologies, created by ISACA (the Information Systems Audit and Control Association), is a framework designed to help organizations govern and manage information technology (IT) effectively. It provides a comprehensive set of best practices and control objectives that organizations can use to

- **Align IT with Business Goals:** COBIT emphasizes the importance of ensuring that IT investments support the overall business strategy of the organization.

- **Manage IT Risks:** The framework helps organizations identify, assess, and manage IT-related risks.

- **Improve IT Governance:** COBIT provides guidance on establishing a robust IT governance structure with clear roles and responsibilities.

- **Optimize IT Processes:** It outlines best practices for managing various IT processes, such as IT service delivery, security, and resource management.

The key characteristics of COBIT:

Process-Oriented: COBIT focuses on IT processes rather than specific technologies.

Control Objectives: It provides a set of high-level and detailed control objectives that organizations can use to measure their IT governance maturity.

Risk-Based: COBIT encourages organizations to take a risk-based approach to IT governance, focusing on areas with the highest potential impact.

Non-prescriptive: The framework doesn't dictate specific tools or technologies, allowing organizations to customize it to their needs.

There are three main benefits of using COBIT:

Improved IT Governance: COBIT helps organizations establish a structured approach to managing IT, leading to better decision-making and resource allocation.

Enhanced Risk Management: By identifying and addressing IT risks proactively, organizations can minimize the potential for disruptions and financial losses.

Increased Efficiency: COBIT promotes best practices for IT processes, leading to improved efficiency and cost savings.

Additionally, implementing COBIT can help organizations demonstrate compliance with various IT and security compliance and regulations, such as PCI-DSS, HIPAA, SOX, and ISO 27001. COBIT is a valuable resource for organizations of all sizes and industries seeking to improve their IT governance and management practices.

It should also be noted that COBIT can be used in conjunction with other IT frameworks and standards, such as ITIL and ISO/IEC 27001.

5.8 Australian Government Protective Security Policy Framework (PSPF)

The Australian Government Protective Security Policy Framework (PSPF) is a set of policies and guidelines designed to help Australian Government entities safeguard their people, information, and assets, both domestically and internationally. It acts as a road map for robust government cybersecurity and physical security practices.

The key aspects of the PSPF include

Protecting People, Information, and Assets: The PSPF emphasizes the importance of securing these three critical elements for effective government operations.

Maturity Model: The framework encourages a progressive approach, allowing entities to implement security measures at a level appropriate to their risk profile.

The PSPF also has clearly defined goals encompassing

Security Governance: Establishes clear roles, responsibilities, and oversight mechanisms for information and physical security within government entities.

Information Security: Provides guidance on managing information assets securely, including data classification, access controls, and incident response.

Personnel Security: Ensures that personnel working with sensitive government information and assets meet appropriate security clearances and trustworthiness standards.

Physical Security: Outlines best practices for securing physical locations, assets, and infrastructure.

The benefits of adopting the PSPF include an improved security posture, and by implementing the PSPF, government entities can significantly strengthen their overall security posture and reduce the risk of cyberattacks, data breaches, and physical security incidents.

It also facilitates enhanced compliance, aligning with various Australian government security regulations and standards, facilitating compliance efforts, and ensuring a consistent approach to security across all government entities. It is also focused on risk-based management. The PSPF allows entities to tailor their security measures based on their specific risks and priorities.

It's important to note that the PSPF is primarily intended for Australian Government departments, agencies, and statutory authorities. However, the principles and best practices outlined in the framework can also be valuable for nongovernment organizations (NGOs) and businesses that work closely with the government.

5.9 Real-World Example – EnergyAustralia

EnergyAustralia, a major player in Australia's energy sector, dodged a data breach bullet in late 2022 thanks to their dedication to robust cybersecurity practices. This example shines a light on how adopting security frameworks, specifically the Essential Eight, can significantly strengthen an organization's cyber defenses.

The close call began with a seemingly ordinary email circulating within EnergyAustralia. The email disguised itself as a legitimate software update notification, complete with a malicious link waiting to be clicked. Luckily, the company's IT team had undergone extensive awareness training based on the Essential Eight's focus on user application hardening (one key component of the E8). This training equipped them to recognize the telltale signs of a phishing attempt. EnergyAustralia's adherence to these strategies played a pivotal role in preventing a potential breach. They implemented the following recommended E8 controls:

Application Hardening: EnergyAustralia followed best practices for software configuration, ensuring their applications were set up securely with unnecessary features disabled. This made them less vulnerable to exploits triggered by clicking malicious links in phishing emails.

Patch Application Vulnerabilities: EnergyAustralia maintained a rigorous patch management program. This program ensured that all software applications were kept up-to-date with the latest security patches. This minimized the potential for attackers to exploit known vulnerabilities in outdated software.

Restrict Administrative Access: EnergyAustralia adhered to the principle of least privilege, granting administrative access only to authorized personnel and for specific tasks. By limiting access, they minimized the potential damage if an attacker managed to gain access to a user account.

Multi-factor Authentication (MFA): EnergyAustralia implemented MFA for critical systems, which significantly reduced the risk of unauthorized access even if an attacker managed to steal login credentials.

By identifying the suspicious email and recognizing the potential threat, the IT team was able to take swift action. They contained the email and prevented it from spreading further within the organization. No employee clicked the malicious link, and no data was compromised.

EnergyAustralia's experience underscores the importance of adopting security frameworks like the Essential Eight. These frameworks provide a structured approach to cybersecurity, outlining key controls that significantly reduce the risk of cyberattacks.

5.10 Prioritizing Framework Adoption

Selecting the most appropriate cybersecurity framework can be a challenge for directors and boards. While all the frameworks discussed offer valuable guidance, some may be better suited to your organization than others. Here are some key factors to consider when deciding which framework to adopt and prioritize:

- **Industry:** Certain industries have specific regulatory requirements or established best practices that may influence framework selection. For example, the **Australian Energy Sector Cyber Security Framework (AESCSF)** is specifically designed for organizations in the energy sector.

- **Size:** Smaller organizations may benefit from a more streamlined framework like the **ACSC Essential Eight**, while larger organizations with complex IT environments might find the **NIST CSF** more comprehensive.

- **Risk Profile:** Organizations handling sensitive data or operating in high-risk sectors should prioritize frameworks that address those specific threats. The **CIS Controls** provide a prioritized list of controls to mitigate common vulnerabilities.

5.11 Key Questions for Your Organization

- Do we understand the difference between cybersecurity frameworks (actionable steps) and governance principles (overarching guidance)?

- Have we chosen and implemented a cybersecurity framework that aligns with our organization's needs and risk profile, such as the ACSC Essential Eight, NIST CSF, or CIS Controls?

- Do we understand the key components and functions of our chosen framework, and have we tailored it to our specific requirements?

- Have we consulted with cybersecurity professionals to guide us in selecting and implementing the most appropriate framework(s) for our organization?

- Do we have a plan for regularly reviewing and updating our chosen framework(s) to adapt to the evolving threat landscape?

- Are we regularly assessing our cybersecurity maturity within the framework and identifying areas for improvement?

- Have we considered using multiple frameworks to address different aspects of our cybersecurity strategy, such as using the Essential Eight for foundational controls and NIST CSF for a broader risk management approach?

- Are we seeking guidance from cybersecurity professionals to ensure effective framework implementation and ongoing maintenance?

5.12 Key Takeaways

This chapter explored the critical role of cybersecurity frameworks in protecting your organization. Here are the key takeaways for this section:

- **Frameworks vs. Governance Principles:** Frameworks provide specific, actionable steps for implementing security measures, while governance principles focus on the overall approach and leadership commitment. Both are essential for a well-rounded cybersecurity strategy.

- **Benefits of Frameworks:** Frameworks offer numerous advantages, including improved security posture, compliance with regulations, effective risk management, standardized practices, and improved communication within the organization.

- **Popular Frameworks:**

  - **ACSC Essential Eight:** Prioritizes mitigation strategies for prevalent cyber threats.

  - **NIST CSF:** Offers a comprehensive framework with five core functions (identify, protect, detect, respond, recover) to manage cybersecurity risk.

  - **CIS Controls:** Provide a prioritized list of best practices to address common vulnerabilities.

- **Additional Frameworks:** The chapter explored other relevant frameworks like the Cloud Controls Matrix (CCM), Australian Energy Sector Cyber Security Framework (AESCSF), COBIT, and the Australian Government Protective Security Policy Framework (PSPF).

- **Selecting the Right Framework:** Consider your industry, organization size, and risk profile when choosing a framework.

- Seek guidance from cybersecurity professionals when selecting and implementing a framework. This can be particularly helpful for directors and boards without a technical background.

References

[15]   www.cyber.gov.au/resources-business-and-government/
        essential-cyber-security/essential-eight

[16]   www.cyber.gov.au/sites/default/files/2023-11/
        PROTECT%20-%20Essential%20Eight%20Maturity%20Model%20
        %28November%202023%29.pdf

[17]   www.nist.gov/cyberframework

[18]   www.cisecurity.org/controls

[19]   https://cloudsecurityalliance.org/research/cloud-
        controls-matrix

[20]   https://aemo.com.au/en/initiatives/major-programs/
        cyber-security/aescsf-framework-and-resources

[21]   www.isaca.org/resources/cobit

PART II

Overseeing Cybersecurity risk: Requirements, Attack Vectors, Strategies and Mitigation Controls

CHAPTER 6

How They Work Together

The relationship between cyber governance and principles, cyber frameworks, controls, and compliance can be understood as a layered approach to cybersecurity within an organization. Here's a breakdown of each element and how they work together:

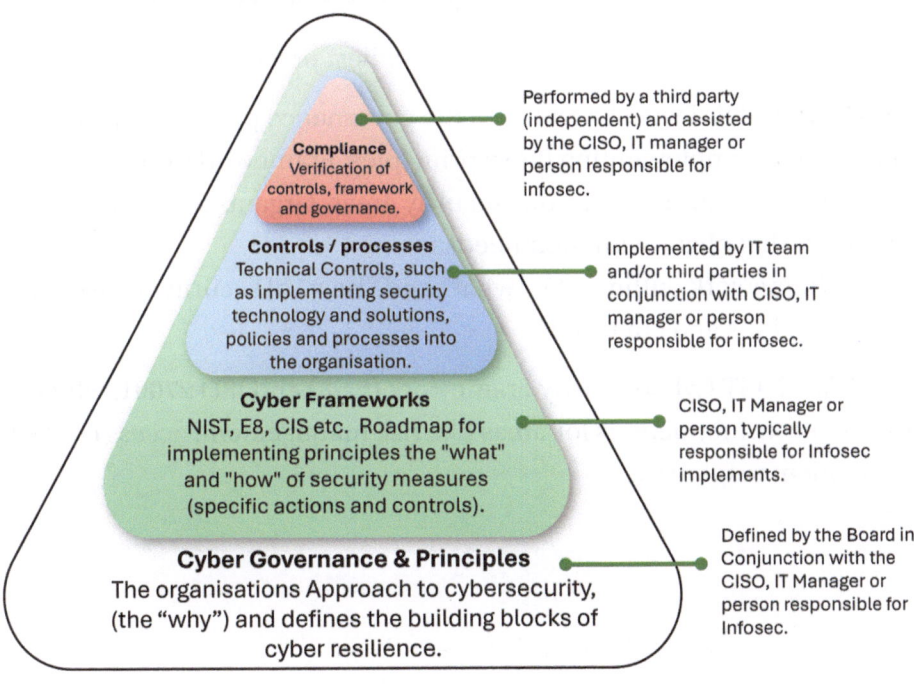

Compliance
Verification of controls, framework and governance.

Performed by a third party (independent) and assisted by the CISO, IT manager or person responsible for infosec.

Controls / processes
Technical Controls, such as implementing security technology and solutions, policies and processes into the organisation.

Implemented by IT team and/or third parties in conjunction with CISO, IT manager or person responsible for infosec.

Cyber Frameworks
NIST, E8, CIS etc. Roadmap for implementing principles the "what" and "how" of security measures (specific actions and controls).

CISO, IT Manager or person typically responsible for Infosec implements.

Cyber Governance & Principles
The organisations Approach to cybersecurity, (the "why") and defines the building blocks of cyber resilience.

Defined by the Board in Conjunction with the CISO, IT Manager or person responsible for Infosec.

6.1 First Layer – Cyber Governance and Principles

Focus: High-level guidance and leadership oversight.

Description: This layer forms the foundation, representing the "why" and overall approach to cybersecurity within an organization. It establishes high-level guidance through principles like risk management, building cyber resilience, and a focus on security awareness.

Examples: AICD Cyber Security Governance Principles emphasize aspects such as board oversight, risk management, and building a culture of cyber resilience.

6.2 Second Layer – Cyber Frameworks

Focus: Provides a structured approach and best practices.

Description: This layer sits on top of the governance principles, providing a road map for implementing those principles. Frameworks offer best practices and controls for various security areas. Organizations choose a framework that aligns with their needs.

The framework outlines the "what" and "how" of security measures (specific actions and controls).

Examples: NIST Cybersecurity Framework (CSF) and ISO 27001, which provide recommendations for areas like risk management, access control, and incident response.

6.3 Third Layer – Controls/Processes

Focus: Implementing technologies, solutions, or policy and process changes within the organization to achieve the requirements outlined in the framework(s).

Description: This layer sits on top of the cybersecurity framework(s) and is the implemented technical controls or solutions and the nontechnical policies and procedures, which support the technology within the organization to achieve the requirements outlined in the framework(s).

Examples: Implementation of regular phishing and awareness training platform for staff (technology), supported by HR and mandated to employees via HR processes (processes and procedures), requiring completion of the training.

6.4 Fourth Layer – Compliance

Focus: Meeting regulatory requirements (compliance).

Description: This layer focuses on meeting legal or regulatory requirements for cybersecurity. It ensures the organization meets minimum security standards. It also dictates specific actions or reporting obligations mandated by regulators. Note that a lot of compliance requirements are just associated with governance, processes, and procedures, not technical controls, which is why it's important to point out that compliance does not equal security.

Examples: ASIC cybersecurity requirements for financial institutions outline mandatory controls or reporting procedures for cyber incidents.

Returning to the same house-building analogy we utilized previously, in the context of these four layers:

Cyber Governance and Principles: The blueprint – defines the overall structure, foundation, and purpose of the house.

Cyber Frameworks: The construction manual – provides specific instructions, codes, and best practices for building the house securely (walls, doors, windows).

Controls/Processes: The building of the house.

Compliance: The building codes and inspection – ensures the house meets minimum safety and regulatory standards.

If we examine how these work together, cyber governance principles set the overall direction for cybersecurity within the organization. Leadership commitment, risk management strategy, and a focus on cyber resilience are established at this level.

Cyber frameworks provide a road map to implement those principles. They offer a structured approach with specific recommendations for security controls, processes, and procedures. Organizations can choose a framework that aligns with their industry and risk profile.

Controls/processes provide the tools, processes, and procedures to implement the controls outlined in the risk framework(s).

Compliance ensures the organization meets any legal or regulatory requirements for cybersecurity. This might involve implementing specific controls mandated by regulations or reporting cybersecurity incidents to relevant authorities.

Some points to consider include the following:

- It's important to remember that cybersecurity frameworks, while valuable, have limitations. They are not a one-size-fits-all solution and may require customization to address an organization's specific needs and threat landscape.

- Frameworks are dynamic documents that can evolve over time. Successful implementation requires ongoing effort to monitor the threat landscape, adapt controls, and adjust the cybersecurity strategy accordingly.

- Compliance with regulations is a baseline requirement, but a strong cybersecurity strategy goes beyond just meeting the minimum.

- Cyber governance principles are an ongoing process, requiring continuous monitoring, adaptation, and improvement of the organization's cybersecurity posture.

By effectively combining these elements, organizations can build a robust and well-rounded cybersecurity strategy that protects their critical assets, fosters a culture of security awareness, and demonstrates their commitment to responsible data management.

6.5 Real-World Example – Qantas

Qantas has had its fair share of cyberattacks over the years. One such attack in 2019 is a perfect example of how the layers we talked about earlier (cyber governance and principles, cyber framework adoption, security controls and processes, and compliance) prevented a potential significant breach.

In 2019, they faced a sophisticated cyberattack targeting the Qantas Frequent Flyer (QFF) program. This program stores a wealth of customer data, including names, contact information, and some credit card details. Qantas had adopted all of the four layers above:

Cyber Governance: Fortunately, Qantas had a robust cyber governance framework in place. This framework outlined clear roles and responsibilities for cybersecurity across the organization. The executive team championed cybersecurity as a top priority, allocating sufficient resources and budget for security measures.

Principles Put to Practice: Qantas embraced several core cybersecurity principles outlined by the Australian Signals Directorate (ASD). These principles focus on four key activities: govern, protect, detect, and respond.

- **Govern:** Qantas had a dedicated security team responsible for managing cyber risks. Regular risk assessments were conducted to identify potential vulnerabilities. This proactive approach helped them stay ahead of emerging threats.

- **Protect:** Qantas implemented a layered security approach, utilizing various security controls and processes. This included firewalls, intrusion detection and prevention systems (IDS/IPS), data encryption, and multi-factor authentication (MFA) for user access. Additionally, they invested in employee security awareness training, educating staff on how to identify and avoid phishing attempts and other social engineering tactics.

- **Detect:** Qantas continuously monitored their network for suspicious activity using sophisticated security monitoring tools. These tools are designed to detect potential breaches in real time.

- **Respond:** Qantas had a well-defined incident response plan in place, outlining the steps to take in case of a cyberattack. This plan ensured a quick and coordinated response to minimize damage.

Cyber Frameworks and Compliance: Qantas also leveraged industry-recommended cyber frameworks, such as the Essential Eight. These frameworks provide best practices for cybersecurity and helped Qantas ensure their security posture was aligned with industry standards. Additionally, Qantas complied with relevant Australian data privacy regulations, such as the Notifiable Data Breaches (NDB) scheme. This compliance ensured that they had robust data security measures in place and clear reporting procedures in case of a breach.

The Outcome: Thanks to their strong cyber governance, commitment to cybersecurity principles, implemented security controls and processes, and compliance with relevant frameworks, Qantas was able to detect the attempted attack on their QFF program in its early stages. They successfully repelled the attack before any customer data was compromised.

Qantas's proactive approach to cybersecurity prevented a potentially damaging data breach, safeguarding the personal information of millions of frequent flyers.

6.6 MITRE ATT&CK

The cybersecurity landscape is constantly evolving, and new frameworks are emerging to address these changes. One such framework is the MITRE ATT&CK framework. Unlike traditional frameworks that focus on specific controls, MITRE ATT&CK focuses on attacker behavior. It catalogs various tactics, techniques, and procedures (TTPs) commonly used by cyber adversaries. By understanding these attacker behaviors, organizations can develop more effective defense strategies.

By incorporating insights from MITRE ATT&CK into the control selection process outlined in your chosen framework (e.g., NIST CSF), you can create a more targeted and threat-informed cybersecurity posture.

6.7 The Role of Threat Intelligence

We will discuss threat intelligence in much more detail in future chapters, but it's important to flag the role of threat intelligence with regard to frameworks and combining it with governance and controls. While cybersecurity frameworks provide a road map, organizations need real-time information about evolving threats to effectively implement those strategies. This is where threat intelligence comes in.

Threat intelligence refers to the analysis of data about cyber threats and actors. This analysis helps organizations understand the:

- **Motives and Capabilities of Attackers:** Identifying who may target your organization and what methods they might use.

- **Emerging Threats and Vulnerabilities:** Staying informed about new attack techniques and recently discovered security weaknesses.

- **Industry Trends and Best Practices:** Learning from the experiences of others in your sector.

By integrating threat intelligence into your cybersecurity strategy, you can:

- **Prioritize Security Controls:** Focus resources on mitigating the threats most likely to impact your organization.

- **Proactive Defense:** Identify and address vulnerabilities before they are exploited.

- **Improved Decision-Making:** Make informed decisions about security investments and incident response procedures.

6.8 Real-World Example – Threat Intelligence

The National Australia Bank (NAB) narrowly avoided a cyber catastrophe in early 2023 thanks to a timely warning from a reliable source of threat intelligence. Threat intelligence equips organizations (like the NAB in this case) to anticipate and prepare for attacks by providing insights into the tactics, techniques, and procedures (TTPs) used by attackers.

In this case, the threat intelligence report detailed a sophisticated phishing campaign designed to steal login credentials from bank employees. These stolen credentials could then be used to access bank accounts and potentially transfer funds. Armed with this knowledge, the NAB security team took immediate action. They launched a targeted awareness campaign, educating employees about the specific phishing tactics described in the threat intelligence report. This proactive education helped employees recognize the phishing attempts and avoid them.

Additionally, the NAB security team implemented additional security measures based on the intelligence report. These measures included strengthening email filtering systems to identify and block suspicious emails and enabling multi-factor authentication (MFA) for all employee accounts.

Weeks later, a wave of phishing emails targeted NAB employees. These emails mimicked the details mentioned in the threat intelligence report, attempting to trick employees into giving away their login credentials. However, due to the proactive awareness campaign and the additional security measures, employees were able to identify the phishing attempts. They avoided clicking malicious links or entering their credentials, effectively rendering the attack unsuccessful. With their data protected, no customer information was compromised.

The NAB experience highlights the critical role of threat intelligence in cyber defense. By utilizing threat intelligence, NAB gained early warning about the impending attack, allowing them to proactively prepare. Additionally, the intelligence report helped focus their defense efforts by providing specific details about the attack's methods. This enabled NAB to tailor their security measures to address the specific threat, ultimately protecting customer data.

NAB's story serves as a testament to the importance of investing in threat intelligence capabilities. Organizations can achieve this by subscribing to threat intelligence feeds, collaborating with industry partners, and even building an internal threat intelligence team. The cyber threat landscape is constantly evolving, so continuous vigilance is essential.

6.9 Key Questions for Your Organization

- Do we understand how cyber governance principles, frameworks, controls, and compliance work together as a layered approach to cybersecurity?

- Do we have a clear set of cyber governance principles that guide our overall approach to cybersecurity? If so, do they align with established frameworks like the AICD Cyber Security Governance Principles?

- As a board, do we actively oversee and understand the implementation of these principles within our organization?

- Do we have a process for regularly reviewing and updating these principles to ensure they remain relevant and effective in the face of evolving cyber threats?

- Have we adopted a recognized cybersecurity framework (e.g., NIST CSF, ISO 27001) that is appropriate for our industry and the level of risk we face?

- Do we, as a board, understand the key components of the chosen framework and how it can be tailored to address our organization's specific needs and risks?

- Are we regularly updated on the implementation progress of the framework and its effectiveness in mitigating cyber risks?

- Have we implemented technical controls (e.g., firewalls, encryption, intrusion detection systems) and nontechnical controls (e.g., policies, procedures, security awareness training) to support our chosen framework(s)?

- Do we have a process in place to ensure these controls are regularly reviewed, updated, and tested for effectiveness against evolving threats?

- Are we receiving regular reports on the effectiveness of these controls and any identified gaps or weaknesses?

- Do we have a clear understanding of the legal and regulatory requirements for cybersecurity that apply to our industry and organization?

- Are we conducting regular compliance audits to verify our adherence to these requirements?

- Do we have a process for promptly addressing any compliance gaps identified in these audits?

- Are we using threat intelligence from sources like the ACSC to inform our cybersecurity strategy, proactively identify and address emerging threats and vulnerabilities, and prioritize controls?

- Are we regularly reviewing and updating our incident response plan to ensure it is effective and aligned with our cybersecurity strategy and current threat landscape?

6.10 Key Takeaways

- Cybersecurity within an organization can be understood as a layered approach involving:

  - **Cyber Governance and Principles:** Sets the overall direction and establishes high-level guidance (e.g., risk management, cyber resilience).

  - **Cyber Framework:** Provides a structured road map for implementing those principles with best practices and control recommendations (e.g., NIST CSF, ISO 27001).

  - **Controls/Processes:** Implements technical and nontechnical solutions to meet the framework requirements.

  - **Compliance:** Ensures the organization meets legal and regulatory requirements (minimum security standards).

- When choosing and implementing a framework

  - Remember that frameworks are not one size fits all. Select a framework that aligns with your industry and risk profile (e.g., NIST for general use, HIPAA for healthcare).

  - Frameworks are dynamic and require ongoing monitoring and adjustments to stay effective.

- Meeting compliance is a baseline, not the ultimate goal. A strong cybersecurity strategy goes beyond minimum requirements.

- Cyber governance principles are an ongoing process. Regularly monitor, adapt, and improve your organization's cybersecurity posture.

- Consider incorporating insights from MITRE ATT&CK, which focuses on attacker behavior, to enhance control selection within your chosen framework.

- Threat intelligence provides real-time information about evolving threats to inform your cybersecurity strategy and prioritize controls.

CHAPTER 7

Understanding Cyber Risk and Cyber Resilience

Okay, so now you understand the differences between cybersecurity governance and principles, frameworks, and how compliance and implementation ties in. As you may have noticed, a lot of the governance principles and standards and cybersecurity frameworks have crossover recommendations. For example, nearly all define requirements for reporting of security events and implementing of end-user education programs.

Now let's put this into more of a checklist of requirements to ensure your organization's cyber resilience and compliance with security best practices. The concepts to be covered in this section are not exhaustive; it's based on my 17+ years of security and penetration testing experience, and there is always more that can be done. From a security standpoint, the more you can do, the better; however, these are the basics you should ensure that your organization has covered to minimize cyber risk and to ensure cyber resilience so that you can quickly and effectively bounce back from an event.

When I'm explaining cyber risk and cyber resilience to boards and senior management within organizations, I break cyber risk up into four main areas, with oversight encompassing two additional areas.

© The Editor(s) (if applicable) and The Author(s),
under exclusive license to APress Media, LLC, part of Springer Nature 2024
D. Weis, *Boardroom Cybersecurity*, https://doi.org/10.1007/979-8-8688-0785-5_7

As a director or board member, you will typically sit in the Oversight and Direction area, with a few overlaps with the sub areas. If you are a chief information security officer (CISO) or IT manager or security person, then all subareas will apply to you with reporting to management (Oversight and Direction).

7.1 Oversight and Direction

This is going to be one of the most important areas that organizations must have covered. It forms the foundation for guidance and assessment of the organizational risk areas and ensures cyber readiness. When board members and directors are making decisions and guiding the organization, it should be proportional to the organization type, the nature of the organization, the complexity of the organization, the industry risk profile, and the sensitivity of data and assets held by the organization.

It's important to note that it is not the board's responsibility to manage cyber risk, but the board is held accountable for ensuring governance and risk mitigation/management.

The Oversight and Direction pillar consists of six areas:

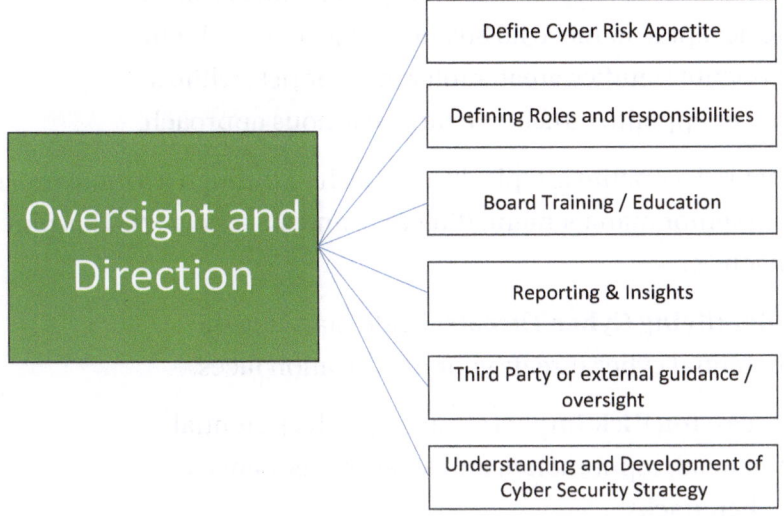

7.1.1 Cyber Risk Appetite

The first component of the Oversight and Direction pillar is the defining of your organizational risk appetite, which should be defined at the board level before anything else.

For those of you new to CRA, cyber risk appetite (or CRA) refers to the amount of cyber risk an organization is willing to accept in pursuit of its business goals. It's essentially a predetermined level of risk that the organization is comfortable tolerating.

It incorporates two key areas:

Risk: The potential for a cyberattack or security incident to occur and cause harm to the organization. This harm could be financial (data breaches, downtime), reputational (loss of customer trust), or legal (regulatory fines).

Appetite: The organization's tolerance for this risk. It reflects the level of risk the organization is willing to accept to achieve its business objectives. A higher appetite signifies greater tolerance for risk, while a lower appetite indicates a more cautious approach.

Cyber risk appetite is typically established through a formal process involving senior management, directors, and stakeholders. This process often involves:

Identifying Cyber Threats: Understanding the potential cyber threats your organization faces.

Assessing Risk Impact: Evaluating the potential financial, reputational, and legal consequences of cyberattacks.

Defining Risk Tolerance: Determining the level of risk the organization is comfortable accepting.

Developing Security Strategy: Creating a cybersecurity strategy that aligns with the defined risk appetite.

Why Is Cyber Risk Appetite Important?

Primarily, it allows for informed decision-making. By defining the cyber risk appetite, organizations can make informed decisions regarding security investments, resource allocation, and risk mitigation strategies. It also helps to balance risk and reward, striking a balance between prioritizing security and enabling business innovation.

Cyber risk appetite can also be used to ensure alignment with business goals. Cybersecurity measures should align with the organization's overall business goals and risk tolerance.

There are a number of factors that typically affect an organization's risk appetite, including:

Industry: Organizations in high-risk industries (finance, healthcare, critical infrastructure) typically have a lower cyber risk appetite due to the sensitivity of the data they handle.

Business Model: Organizations reliant on online operations or handling sensitive data might have a lower tolerance for risk.

Regulatory Requirements: Compliance with industry regulations may influence the level of acceptable cyber risk.

Lastly, cyber risk appetite is not a static concept. It should be reviewed and potentially adjusted periodically based on changes in the organization's business environment, threat landscape, and regulatory requirements.

So we now understand that cyber risk appetite is important, but how do cyber risk appetite and cybersecurity risk and mitigation plans fit into the bigger picture of corporate risk management?

Recall that corporate risk appetite defines the level of risk an organization is willing to accept in pursuit of its goals. The risk management framework, on the other hand, is the structured approach an organization uses to identify, assess, prioritize, and manage all types of risks, including cyber risks. The cybersecurity risk and mitigation plan becomes a key component within this framework. It details the specific risks associated with technology, information, and digital assets, along with strategies to mitigate those risks.

And then we have the business continuity plan (BCP). This plan outlines how an organization will recover from disruptive events, including cyberattacks. The cybersecurity risk and mitigation plan plays a crucial role in informing the BCP. By identifying potential cyber threats and their impact on critical operations, the BCP can incorporate strategies for restoring functionality and minimizing downtime in the event of a cyberattack.

So in terms of how these elements work together:

Identify and Assess Risks: The cybersecurity risk and mitigation plan starts by identifying potential cyber threats, vulnerabilities, and their impact on the organization. This information feeds into the broader risk management framework.

Prioritization and Mitigation: Based on the risk assessment and the organization's risk appetite, the plan prioritizes risks and outlines specific mitigation strategies. These strategies may involve technical controls like firewalls and encryption but also nontechnical measures such as employee training and incident response procedures.

Integration with BCP: The identified cyber threats and their potential impact inform the BCP. The BCP can then incorporate strategies for dealing with these threats, such as data recovery procedures, backup systems, and communication protocols.

By closely aligning the cybersecurity risk and mitigation plan with the corporate risk appetite, risk management framework, and BCP, organizations can create a holistic approach to managing cyber risks and ensuring business continuity in the face of cyber threats. This integrated approach ensures that cybersecurity risks are not considered in isolation but rather as part of the organization's overall risk landscape.

7.1.2 Define Roles and Responsibilities

It's important to define who has responsibility for cybersecurity within the organization. Having clearly defined roles and responsibilities will ensure that directors have sufficient oversight of organizational cyber risk and can effectively make decisions based on that oversight. Although organizations as a whole are responsible for cybersecurity and cyber awareness, there still needs to be a reporting contact and someone providing cybersecurity information back to the board. This person(s) should understand current cyber risk, mitigation strategies, and the threat landscape and understand all operational areas and functions of the business so that they can accurately assess and inform the board on cyber risk, specific to the organization.

If we take the AICD Cyber Security Governance guidelines [22] as an example, they will refer to appointing a "cyber champion" to promote cyber resilience and respond to queries. Typically though, you will find that in a large number of organizations, there may not be a CISO (chief information security officer) or dedicated cybersecurity resource, and in this case, it typically falls back to an IT manager or head of the IT/technology division to provide this visibility and reporting. Additionally, this responsibility may be shared across a number of key personnel, such as the CEO, CTO, or CIO.

On the same token, it is not uncommon for boards to designate a director or group of directors to oversee this function and should also be considered as part of defining these roles and responsibilities. Some organizations may also be required to form subcommittees (such as a risk/audit committee), which I encounter quite often within organizations, which can effectively bridge the gap between the management/executive team for the organization (such as C-level staff) and the board from a reporting and risk management perspective, although this is more common with larger organizations as opposed to SMEs.

Lastly, these defined roles and responsibilities should be reviewed periodically to ensure that they continue to remain effective within the constantly evolving cybersecurity space. The board should also consider these responsibilities and ensure backup resources are in place if key staff leave the organization.

7.1.3 Board Training/Education

As the threat landscape is constantly changing and evolving, the board should ensure that they are staying ahead of and discussing current and emerging threats. In an ideal world, this would typically be the responsibility of the defined "cybersecurity champion(s)" or person(s) responsible for reporting on cybersecurity to bring current and emerging threats and risks to the attention of the board, but it is still key for directors to be across the ever-changing threat landscape. This may involve periodic presentations from external cyber risk/cybersecurity experts, or specific focused training for directors at periodic intervals, facilitated by external parties, and staying abreast of current security threats via security news emails, websites, blogs, and webinars.

All directors should feel comfortable with basic cybersecurity concepts and basic cybersecurity risk mitigation strategies to make an accurate determination and assessment of cyber risk and to guide organizational decision-making. I have seen cases where, as part of the cyber risk/cybersecurity reporting to the board each month/quarter, a list of current and emerging threats and trends is presented, which not only educates the board but can then be considered in the context of risk mitigation measures and decisions for the organization.

Similarly, the board should ensure that all people responsible for cybersecurity within the organization are frequently undertaking training and attending events and webinars to boost their awareness and knowledge of cybersecurity and the threat landscape.

7.1.4 Reporting

Regular, clear reporting on cybersecurity is essential for board members to understand how well the organization's controls, processes, and staff are building cyber resilience. Management should present these reports to the board or a dedicated committee for discussion each month.

It's important that reports are focusing on insights and not just numbers. Reports should align with the organization's cyber strategy and go beyond basic numbers and metrics, such as the number of emails blocked or number of endpoint malware detections, and should be measured.

They should provide information about internal and external threats, results from any recent audits, compliance checks, penetration testing, or vulnerability assessment results and should also include broader cyber trends relevant to the organization.

All information should be presented in layman's terms, that is, not overly technical or using complex technical jargon, to foster better communication and engagement. The data presented should also encompass trending data and how effective recent risk mitigation strategies or security technology implementations are performing in reducing the organization's overall risk profile.

At a minimum, the report should be providing the following information and metrics:

- Staff awareness training and completion rates.

- Results from regular phishing campaigns/simulations.

- SOC (security operations center) or security vendor incidents detected, how they were responded to, and how they benchmarked against previous months/periods. This should also encompass staff-related incidents.

- Lessons learned from any recent incidents.

- An update on cybersecurity initiatives and cyber strategy performance.

- Results from monthly vulnerability scans and internal audits/compliance assessments.

- Results from external penetration testing or audit activities.

- Remediation activities and results from vulnerability scans and pentest reports.

- The effectiveness of current cybersecurity practices.

- Information on current cybersecurity trends and security threats, which can be sourced from or combined with intelligence and alerts from industry and the government such as the ACSC.

7.1.5 Third-Party Guidance/Oversight

It's important for directors to understand the value and limits of external cybersecurity expertise. Firstly, it is a good idea to incorporate external insights into periodic reporting to the board. It should be noted that while external cybersecurity experts offer valuable insights and support, building internal capabilities remains crucial for long-term cyber resilience.

There are a number of benefits associated with external expertise including:

Fresh Perspective: Independent experts can provide an objective view of the organization's cyber risk posture and identify potential blind spots.

Incident Response: During a cyberattack, external experts can be a critical resource for immediate response and recovery efforts.

Validation: Independent experts can provide validation of existing data presented to the board and validation of existing or newly implement security controls/technologies.

However, it is important for directors to understand that overreliance on external expertise can also be a pitfall. To strike a balance, I would recommend:

Management Training: Invest in training and upskilling of management to understand and manage cyber risks effectively.

Director Education: Educate board members on their role in cybersecurity oversight, empowering them to ask informed questions and hold management accountable.

By combining internal expertise with the strategic use of external consultants, organizations can achieve a more robust and sustainable approach to cybersecurity.

7.1.6 Understanding and Development of a Cybersecurity Strategy

The last component in the Oversight and Direction pillar is the understanding and development of a cybersecurity strategy. The board has a fundamental responsibility to oversee the organization's overall well-being, including its cybersecurity posture. A robust cybersecurity strategy, developed in conjunction with key stakeholders within the organization, demonstrates proactive risk management and helps ensure the organization's continued success. In the context of the board, a cyber strategy specifically:

Provides Insight: Regular reports based on the strategy keep the board informed about cyber risks, vulnerabilities, and the effectiveness of implemented controls.

Facilitates Informed Decisions: The strategy equips the board to make informed decisions regarding resource allocation for cybersecurity initiatives.

Enhances Oversight: The board can leverage the strategy to hold management accountable for upholding a strong cybersecurity posture.

Mitigates Risk: A well-defined strategy demonstrates proactive risk management, potentially reducing the impact of cyberattacks and associated financial losses.

Best Practices for Developing a Cybersecurity Strategy

Building a robust cybersecurity strategy requires a proactive and collaborative approach. Key best practices when developing a strategy include:

Conduct a Thorough Risk Assessment

Identify Critical Assets: The foundation of any good security strategy is understanding what needs to be protected. This includes data, systems, infrastructure, and intellectual property. Also, understand where third-party suppliers come into play, and identify risks and threats associated with the use of key third parties.

Analyze Threats and Vulnerabilities: Research common cyber threats relevant to your industry and the specific vulnerabilities within your organization's systems and processes.

Evaluate Potential Impact: Assess the potential consequences of a cyberattack on your operations, finances, and reputation. This helps prioritize risk mitigation efforts.

Define Clear Security Objectives

Align with Business Goals: Ensure your cybersecurity strategy supports your overall business objectives. Don't implement security measures for the sake of security alone.

Define Desired Outcomes: Clearly define what you want to achieve with your cybersecurity measures. Examples include protecting sensitive data, ensuring system uptime, or achieving compliance with industry regulations.

Leverage Established Frameworks

Take a Standardized Approach: Consider using established cybersecurity frameworks like the NIST Cybersecurity Framework (CSF) or CIS Controls as discussed previously. These frameworks offer a structured approach to implementing best practices and controls.

Flexibility: Don't be afraid to adapt these frameworks to your organization's specific needs and risk profile. They provide a road map, not a one-size-fits-all solution.

Implement a Layered Defense

Ensure You Are Leveraging Multiple Controls: Relying on a single security measure is a recipe for disaster. Implement a layered defense with a combination of controls like access controls, data encryption, security awareness training, and network defense technologies.

Defense in Depth: Structure your controls with a "defense in depth" approach. This means having multiple layers of security so that if one layer is breached, others can still provide protection.

Prioritize Incident Response and Recovery

Prepare for the Inevitable: Cyberattacks are not a matter of "if" but "when." Develop a comprehensive incident response plan that outlines how your organization will identify, contain, manage, eradicate, and recover from a cyberattack.

Test and Refine: Do not let your incident response plan gather dust on a shelf. Regularly test and refine your plan to ensure its effectiveness via incident simulations.

Foster a Culture of Security Awareness

Empower Your Employees: Employees are often the first line of defense against cyberattacks. Invest in security awareness training to educate them on cyber threats, best practices, and how to identify suspicious activity.

Phishing and Social Engineering: Make employees aware of common phishing and social engineering tactics used by attackers. Regular training and phishing simulations can help them identify and avoid these attacks.

Communication and Engagement: Foster a culture of sharing near misses and learning from others.

Continuous Monitoring and Improvement

Stay Ahead of Threats: The cyber threat landscape is constantly evolving. Regularly monitor your systems and networks for vulnerabilities and emerging threats.

Adapt and Improve: As your organization and the threat landscape change, your cybersecurity strategy needs to adapt as well. Conduct periodic risk assessments to identify new vulnerabilities and update your strategy accordingly.

Board Engagement and Communication

Board Oversight: The board has a responsibility to oversee the organization's cybersecurity posture. The board should remain engaged throughout the strategy development process. Regular reporting based on the strategy is essential to keep the board informed on the effectiveness of the strategy, to keep them informed on cyber risks, and to ensure accountability.

Clear Communication: Use clear and concise language when communicating cybersecurity risks and strategies to the board. Avoid overly technical jargon that might hinder their understanding.

By following these best practices and fostering a culture of security awareness, organizations can develop a robust cybersecurity strategy that effectively addresses cyber threats and safeguards their critical assets. Remember, cybersecurity is an ongoing process, not a one-time fix. Continuous monitoring, adaptation, and improvement are key to maintaining a strong security posture in today's ever-evolving digital landscape.

7.1.7 Key Questions for Your Organization

- Have we defined our organization's cyber risk appetite in a way that aligns with our overall business objectives and risk tolerance?

- Are our security objectives clearly defined and aligned with business goals?

- Have we conducted a thorough risk assessment to identify critical assets and potential threats?

- Do we conduct regular risk reduction activities such as penetration testing and vulnerability scanning?

- Does our cybersecurity strategy incorporate established frameworks (e.g., NIST CSF, CIS Controls, etc.) and a layered defense approach?

- Have we implemented a layered defense strategy with access controls (like multi-factor authentication and least privilege), encryption, security awareness training, and robust detection and response mechanisms (like a SIEM or outsourced SOC)?

- Have we fostered or are we fostering a culture of security awareness among our employees through regular training, phishing simulations, and communication of best practices?

- Do we have a well-defined and tested incident response plan that outlines procedures for identifying, containing, and recovering from cyberattacks? Is it regularly tested and updated?

- Are we continuously monitoring and improving our security posture by adapting to the evolving threat landscape and staying informed about emerging threats and vulnerabilities?

- Have we considered cyber insurance as part of our risk management strategy to mitigate financial losses in the event of a cyberattack?

7.2 People

In my opinion, people are the largest cybersecurity risk–facing organizations and are an important component of reducing an organization's cyber risk profile and ensuring cyber resilience. In a large number of penetration testing engagements, I find that organizations are relatively secure from the perimeter and cloud front (as defenses and best practices have advanced over time, so too have organizations), but a simple email-based attack usually bypasses some of the most heavily fortified environments and provides me an opportunistic entry point into the organization.

The People pillar consists of four attack vectors and six mitigation controls:

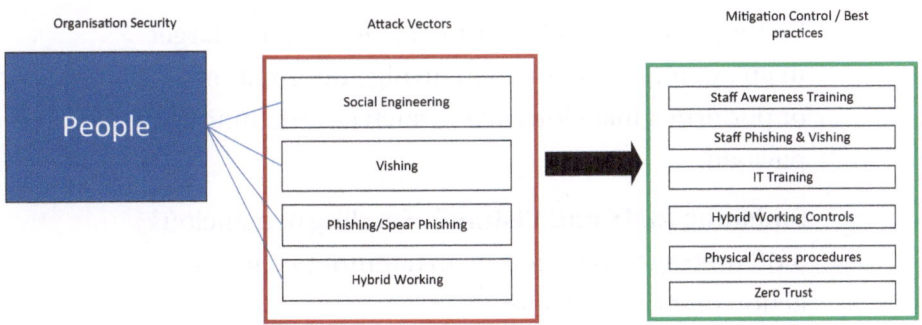

7.2.1 Attack Vectors Targeting People

The first method (which is also part of the next two attack methods) is called social engineering. All attacks that target individuals and people within businesses leverage some form of social engineering. Social engineering is otherwise known as the "art of deception" and is basically where an attacker will convince someone to do something, to click a link, to open an attachment, or to give out some other sensitive information, basically to influence a person to take action that may or may not be in their best interest.

Social engineering has been around for a very long time; it's easy to orchestrate and continues to work time and time again.

Unfortunately, there is no computer system on earth that does not rely on people in one way or another, and social engineering completely bypasses all information controls and goes directly after the weakest link, of course being humans.

Typical attacks targeting organizations include:

- **Phishing:** Generic email phishing targeting a number of staff, usually with the goal of harvesting credentials.

- **Spear Phishing:** Targeted phishing designed to fly under the radar and convince the target to execute an action.

- **Vishing (Voice and Phishing):** Calling up the target in an attempt to get them to divulge information or perform a malicious action such as executing a payload.

- **Smishing (SMS and Vishing):** Sending of malicious SMS messages to targets in an attempt to elicit an action or visit a website.

- **Physical Access Attacks:** Masquerading as an employee or trusted persons to physically access an office/location and access systems (I have a lot of success with this method when conducting penetration tests).

- **Exploitation of Hybrid Working:** For example, users using home machines that may not be as secure or well protected as organizational assets.

- **Financial Fraud Using AI:** We are now starting to see a large number of attacks leveraging AI and deepfakes [23][24], whereby staff are contacted by attackers using AI and deepfakes to imitate legitimate staff, such as the CEO, and coerce the target into making a payment.

Social engineers use many different techniques to convince people to do what they want. Steve Riley has one of the oldest and best presentations out there on Defending Layer 8 [25], and I highly recommend it. Steve identifies a number of types of "exploits" which I can confirm work great for me on penetration testing engagements often, and I've incorporated his presentation into my training for testers and ethical hackers.

Special Consideration for Board Members and Senior Staff
Also worth noting here is that as a board member or director for an organization, you will be frequently targeted by attackers. Senior leaders are prime targets for cybercriminals. Why? Because they often have access to sensitive information and financial resources (such as payments). Attackers might directly target your accounts, or they could try to impersonate you through emails that appear legitimate. These business email compromise (or BEC) scams exploit employees' hesitation to question requests from someone high-ranking.

The best way to mitigate this is through strong security policies, fostering a culture of open communication where employees feel empowered to report suspicious activity, establishing well-defined procedures for reporting suspected BEC attempts and other attacks, and most importantly minimizing your personal digital footprint by being mindful of the personal information you share online and how it can be used to impersonate you in other attacks.

7.2.2 Real-World Example – Attacks Against People

I'm frequently engaged to utilize attacks such as phishing and vishing against staff within an organization as part of penetration testing engagements. Typically, I will set up a fictitious website, such as a new portal or "archiving system" or a clone of another site such as Microsoft 365, and send a convincing email advising the user to visit the website and log in to set up their account. On most engagements, my phishing rate varies from 10% all the way to as high as 70%, based on the level of awareness, staff training, and processes in place. Typically, the number of requests to the helpdesk also varies greatly, with most organizations reporting of a phishing email from staff sitting ~10%, which leaves a lot of non-identified, compromised accounts that the IT team is not aware of.

Another similar tactic I like to use is calling up staff (vishing). If an organization has a good grasp on phishing attacks, I'll call up a staff member, advise them that I'm from IT, and tell them that we are currently setting up a new device (computer) for them. (Staff love getting new devices!) Then I'll state that to complete the setup, I just need their username and password, which nearly every time they will provide. Humans are always the weakest links, and attackers (and testers) will frequently seek to utilize attacks targeting people over typical technology-based attacks.

7.2.3 Mitigating People Risk

This risk area is one of the easiest to remediate if done effectively. The goal of management and directors is to foster a culture of cybersecurity, resilience, and awareness across the organization. Promote cybersecurity, put posters up around the office, discuss cybersecurity topics at team meetings and events, run cybersecurity competitions, and challenge and incentivize your employees to do and be better when it comes to cybersecurity. Additionally, you should be promoting cybersecurity so that it is seen as a business enabler, not a blocker or hindrance.

At the end of the day, the entire organization from the board and directors down to the employees is responsible for building, empowering, and fostering a cyber-resilient organization. Senior management and leadership should actively promote cybersecurity as a core organizational value.

The first mitigation measure should be to implement a scheduled awareness training and phishing program for all staff. It is recommended that you adopt a micro-learning approach (and solution) for staff. This entails the staff completing a short five-to-six-minute video each month with a quiz on a different cybersecurity topic. The old traditional approach of doing a long one-hour annual or biannual training approach doesn't work; within a few weeks of the training, employees have generally forgotten everything, and you are back to square one, as opposed to a micro-learning solution that consistently keeps people engaged in cybersecurity topics. Where possible, it's a good idea to implement some gamification that can incorporate elements of competition, rewards, and badges to motivate employees to learn about cybersecurity best practices.

To this end, whatever solution you implement for the organization should have *engaging* content; an awareness training program that is not engaging will also fall on deaf ears.

Equally important is educating users on cybersecurity and cyber threats at home, such as phishing, scams, social media attacks, secure shopping and payments, etc. We know that staff who are cybersecurity savvy at home will typically use the same methods and be more cautious at work. It also reinforces to staff that as an organization, you care about their "online welfare" once they go home at the end of the day.

Also consider how the training program will be monitored, enforced, and reported to the board and key stakeholders.

Complementing the awareness training piece, the second half entails regular phishing of the staff. It is recommended that you phish your staff monthly. Each month, a phishing email should be sent to all staff encompassing a different domain and scenario and, where possible, tailored to the teams and the technology in use within the organization. For example, if you are using Xero in your finance team, a Xero phish would be perfectly targeted to that team, or an M365 phish targeted to the entire organization. Similar to the training, the phishing program should be monitored and reported to the board and key stakeholders within the organization, and high-risk departments and users (or repeat offenders) should be monitored and receive more targeted training and additional phishing campaigns.

Processes and procedures also play a part here; for example, all organizations should have a documented process for handling payments and invoices and verifying suspect emails. Similarly, the organization should have documented processes and procedures to mitigate the risk of physical access attacks, such as verifying the credentials/ID of unknown personnel, escorting of visitors within secure areas, not leaving visitors unattended, etc.

Technology obviously plays a part here as another backup layer to protect the organization in the event of a slipup. Having a layered approach to security will safeguard the assets when a slipup happens. We're all human, things happen – a person with a newborn who has been

114

up all night as an example, will be tired and much more likely to execute a phishing link as they will be distracted and fatigued. It is near impossible to drive the people risk (like all cyber risks) to zero. Some technological safeguards and measures to protect from people incidents include:

- **Email Filtering:** Limiting the ability of malicious emails to be received

- **Web Filtering and Firewalls:** Limiting which websites can be accessed and what traffic can be permitted

- **Multi-factor Authentication (MFA):** To limit an adversary's login ability if credentials are harvested

- **Alerting, Detection, and Response Mechanisms/ Solutions:** For example, a SOC or security provider providing overwatch and incident response

- **Endpoint Protection on Devices and Phones:** For example, an EDR/XDR product (used to be called antivirus in the old days)

- **Application Whitelisting:** To limit what applications can be run by employees

- **Access Control:** Restricting employees only to the data necessary to complete their roles

- **Implementing Limits:** Implementing limits on social media and personal email usage

This is also where the cybersecurity frameworks come into play, for example, almost all of the above safeguards are recommended (and required) in the ACSC Essential Eight, along with macro security and backups.

7.2.4 Mitigating Risks Associated with Hybrid Working

Hybrid working is typically the norm now across nearly all professions (except emergency services), which in turn presents its own set of risks to the organization. Hybrid working allows for a myriad of productivity benefits to both the organization and individuals alike; however, hybrid working does come with inherent risks. The main risks associated with hybrid working are:

- Compromise of company data via people accessing this data on personal devices, which may not be as secure as company-issued devices. For example, a home device may be running without EDR (endpoint detection and response), may be downloading and running malicious software on the device, and is running high-risk technologies or operating systems, which are now end-of-life.

- Possible information disclosure, people saving organizational data outside of the organization (such as to the hard drive on a home PC), which is then exposed through another attack, such as theft of a device or a malware infection.

- Risks to company infrastructure or cloud services via ransomware and malware attacks. If a user is connected to the company VPN on their home device and this device is not running EDR, and the user inadvertently infects their device with ransomware or malware, then that malware has network connectivity to the organization's infrastructure, allowing for propagation of malware and ransomware to the organizations' assets.

- Unauthorized access to data. Often employees may share their devices with other household members such as kids, family, and housemates, which also then exposes the organization's data to potential unauthorized access.

In my experience, the traditional concept of network zones for an organization, such as external networks, internal networks, demilitarized zones (DMZ), etc., has predominantly gone the way of the dodo when it comes to employees. These zones still exist from an IT infrastructure perspective; however, as employees now access organizational data on any device, from any location, at any time all via cloud services such as Microsoft 365 or Google G-Suite, the concept of network zones no longer applies.

What then are the best methods to mitigate risks associated with hybrid working? The most effective method is to ensure that staff are provided with company-issued devices in the first instance, which then enforces all the required organizational security requirements on the user before accessing company data. Next, the organization should be enforcing policies on employees, to set a minimum number of standards (safeguards) required on personal devices before access to organizational data is granted; for example, users should be running the latest Windows operating system, running endpoint protection software, have a firewall enabled, etc. This should be supplemented with other security technology for personal devices, such as mobile device management (MDM), mobile application management (MAM), and data loss prevention (DLP) solutions; we will discuss these technologies in later sections.

The next mitigation technique involves the organization adopting a Zero Trust model [26], which is recommended for all organizations. A Zero Trust security model more effectively adapts to the complexity of the modern working environment, embracing the hybrid workplace, and protects people, devices, applications, and data wherever they are located.

Today, users access organizational (and their own) data from any device, at any time, all delivered via the cloud, so a Zero Trust model ensures that whichever way a user chooses to work, the access and data is secured from unauthorized access.

To put it in layman's terms, imagine your organization's security like a guarded fortress. Traditionally, everyone inside the walls (the network) was trusted. Zero Trust flips this approach. It assumes anyone accessing data, regardless of location or device (phone, laptop, etc.), could be a threat. Security measures are put in place to verify their identity and access rights for each request, acting like a vigilant guard who constantly checks everyone's credentials.

Zero Trust is now the recommended best practice for all organizations as people work everywhere. With the rise of remote work and cloud computing, employees access data from various locations and devices. Zero Trust secures access no matter where or how they work.

Zero Trust focuses on "never trust, always verify," which constantly confirms someone's identity and right to access data before granting it, minimizing the risk of unauthorized access.

The benefits of adopting Zero Trust include:

Stronger Protection: Reduces the impact of breaches by limiting access and preventing attackers from moving laterally within the system.

Improved Visibility: Provides better insights into what is happening in your systems, allowing for better threat detection and prevention.

Examples of Zero Trust are MFA (multi-factor authentication) and the principle of least privilege access, giving users only the minimum access needed to do their jobs, and data encryption, which protects sensitive data even if it's accessed by unauthorized users.

Budget-Conscious Organizations and Zero Trust

It is important to note that budget-conscious organizations may not be in a position to implement all Zero Trust components right away. If for some reason your IT team cannot implement Zero Trust entirely, they should focus on implementing IAM (Identity Access Management) [27][28] and PAM (Privileged Access Management) [29] combined with technologies such as auditing and logging and awareness training to achieve similar results. This includes:

> **Strengthening Authentication:** Implement multi-factor authentication (MFA) and strong password policies within IAM to make it harder for attackers to gain access to accounts.

> **Segment Access:** Use IAM to control access to different resources based on user roles and needs.

> **Limit Privileged Users:** Implement PAM to restrict access to privileged accounts and monitor their activity closely.

7.2.5 Real-World Example – Hybrid Working Attack

Last year, I was contacted by an organization that required assistance with a ransomware outbreak. The IT team cleaned up the initial outbreak and restored data, but then the organization was continually being reinfected, and they could not identify why or how this was happening. All of their machines had endpoint protection (they were locked down), and they were enforcing tight passwords and MFA; their machines were being wiped (formatted) if they were detected as being infected, so how was this happening?

After investigation, it was found that a staff member working from home was in fact the culprit. The organization did not define any minimum requirements for staff accessing their network over a VPN. The staff member had a single home PC, which was shared with other household members (a risk in itself). Earlier that day, this user's son had been using the device at home, downloading software off torrents and visiting high-risk websites. Somewhere in these activities, he had downloaded and installed some malicious software that executes ransomware once it detected that company network drives were connected. When the staff member connected her VPN and created a connection into the company network, the network drives connected (to allow her access to data), and the ransomware deployed, encrypting all files on the network and spreading through the network using her credentials to log into other systems. Every time this user would connect (after IT cleaned up), it would repeat the process. It wasn't until the organization cut off the VPN temporarily that the true cause was identified. Had the organization adopted requirements for hybrid working, such as issuing company devices or having a predefined set of policies for BYOD (bring your own device), this could have been avoided. And there is nothing to say that the data was not also exfiltrated from the company network to be used in extortion attacks (prior to the encrypting of the files).

7.2.6 Key Questions for Your Organization

- Do all employees receive regular, engaging security awareness training on topics like phishing, social engineering, and password hygiene?

- Are phishing simulations conducted monthly to test employee awareness and identify areas for improvement?

- Are we fostering information sharing across our organization with regard to cyber threats and attacks?

- Are there specific security policies and controls in place for employees working remotely or in a hybrid model, such as VPN requirements, secure access to company data, and device security measures?

- Are company-issued devices provided, or are there clear BYOD (bring your own device) policies that outline security expectations for personal devices used for work?

- Is a Zero Trust security model implemented to secure access regardless of location or device?

7.3 Process and IT Functions

The next pillar of cyber risk and resilience is the Process and IT Functions, which encompasses the internal functions and processes for the organization that reduce overall risk. In general, IT and business processes and procedures standardize and ensure efficiency within the organization, improve overall cybersecurity, reduce risk, result in better communication and collaboration, allow scalability and growth, and ensure compliance. In essence, processes and procedures act as the foundation for a well-run and secure IT environment.

Although typically not something that would be discussed at a board level (more an IT manager function), it is important to understand process and procedure failings, which can contribute to an increased overall risk profile for the organization.

The Process and IT Functions area consists of five attack vectors and five standard mitigation controls:

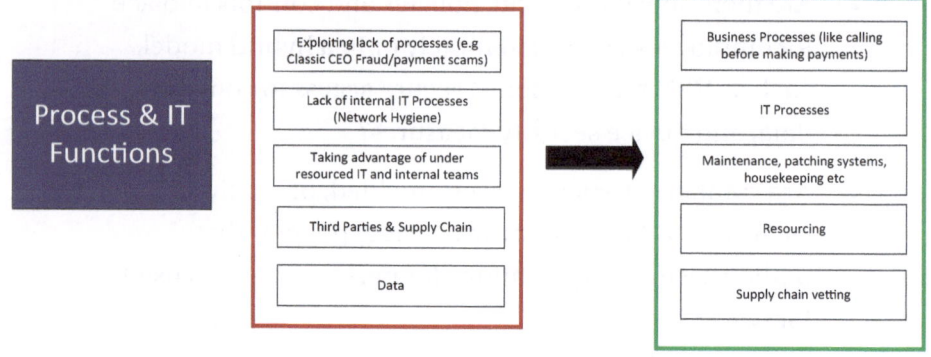

7.3.1 Attack Vectors Targeting Process and IT Functions

Common attack vectors that target organizations include the exploiting of a lack of internal processes; for example, in typical payment scam attacks (CEO fraud), where an employee is contacted and advised to make a payment or transfer, orchestrated from a masqueraded person (such as AI using deepfake or a legitimate-looking email), which is leveraging social engineering tactics, the attacker(s) is relying on a lack of internal processes in place to verify payments to vendors and accounts when requested by the CEO or senior management. The same applies to attacks such as physical access attacks (discussed in the last section), where an attacker is relying on there being no defined and followed processes and procedures to verify the identity of visitors.

7.3.2 Lack of Internal IT Processes and Procedures

The next main attack vector is from a lack of internal IT processes and procedures, what we refer to as network hygiene. During penetration testing engagements, I often encounter organizations with missing network hygiene practices. For example, I often encounter a lot of legacy or stale accounts left in the network that are utilizing weak passwords, and more often than not, these are administrative accounts that provide an easy privilege escalation avenue. These missing hygiene practices extend to offboarding processes that are not in place or not followed correctly and no defined processes for regular patch management of systems and firmware for devices and legacy technology usage. All are easily remediated through the implementation of documented processes and guidelines for the IT team and regular reviews to ensure they are current and being adhered to.

7.3.3 Underresourced Teams

The next attack vector is via the exploitation of underresourced IT and security teams, again an area that I commonly leverage during engagements to bypass detection. IT teams are busy, and often they are also tasked with organizational security. When overutilized and underresourced, attackers can find opportunities to slip past the radar using diversionary tactics. For example, we have seen in a number of data breaches in the past that an attacker will launch ransomware in one part of the network, and while all of the IT team are scrambling to deal with that outbreak, the attacker(s) are actually performing other nefarious activities in a different part of the network. Attackers are also relying on the fact that people go home at night. I know that I often have the most success laterally moving through company networks after 6 p.m. when all of the IT/security team have gone home (if they are not utilizing an outsourced SOC of course).

The next high-risk area for most organizations is the use of third parties and the supply chain, and this has a direct correlation to data management and who has access to organizational data.

7.3.4 Real-World Example – Helpful IT People That Are Underresourced and Missing IT Processes

Recently, I was performing an engagement for a very large retailer. This client had, what I would consider, an underresourced IT team; there were three to four people on the helpdesk supporting approximately 350 users. Along with the resource constraints, they were missing a number of key IT processes, mainly associated with regularly cleaning up accounts (I found they had hundreds of old legacy accounts with some accounts going back as far as 2015 that were active) and had no processes in place to vet user requests.

On this engagement, I was tasked with trying to coerce the helpdesk to perform some actions on a user's account, which would provide me access into their network. I already had some credentials to access a user's account in M365, but I needed access to their internal network and infrastructure using this account (as they had a VPN with MFA setup). I contacted the helpdesk and utilized social engineering techniques to convince the helpdesk staff member that I was the user; I dropped names of others in the organization, for example, "my boss blah," and advised them that I had set up the right software (I found VPN documentation in their SharePoint library) and that I had to get a report out urgently today, but my MFA was not working and I needed it reset. I had access to the user's mailbox, so I could also send them an email if they needed verification. As the helpdesk was very busy, and that I "seemed" to be legit through their discussions with me, I was not vetted further, and the MFA was reset. I then re-setup the MFA to my phone (rather than the users) and logged into the account via the VPN, providing me access to all customer data within the internal networks and services. Had IT been better resourced with more time to spend with me as a user and had clear processes in place for verifying an employee's identity, there is a good chance this attack would have been unsuccessful.

I've performed similar attacks in other engagements where I have managed to get passwords reset for users and even managed to get IT team members to compromise their own device and account! I've had success using these tactics many times in the past.

7.3.5 Lack of Supply Chain Vetting

Now more than ever, supply chain vetting is an absolute must for all organizations. There have been a large number of supply chain attacks over the last five years, such as the SolarWinds Attack (2020), the Kaseya Supply Chain Attack (2021), and the MOVEit Software Attack (2023).

If we take the MOVEit data breach as an example, this was a significant example of a cybercrime supply chain attack. In May 2023, Progress Software, the developer of MOVEit, disclosed a critical SQL injection vulnerability in MOVEit Transfer and MOVEit Cloud (CVE-2023-34362). This vulnerability allowed attackers to gain unauthorized access to a MOVEit server and potentially steal sensitive data transferred through the software.

This vulnerability was quickly exploited by the notorious Clop ransomware gang. Unlike their usual tactics of encrypting data and demanding a ransom, Clop opted for a data extortion approach in this instance.

If we look at this example from the impact on the supply chain, MOVEit was a popular managed file transfer software used by organizations in various sectors, including healthcare, finance, and government. The breach impacted a vast number of organizations (just over 1000) directly and indirectly, as this software was part of their data transfer workflows. Estimates suggest tens of millions of individuals were affected by the stolen data.

The MOVEit breach serves as a stark reminder of the vulnerabilities within the software supply chain. Organizations often rely on trusted vendors for critical services, but those vendors themselves can be targeted by cybercriminals. This incident underscores the importance of understanding a vendor's security posture and implementing additional security measures to mitigate risks.

7.3.6 Real-World Example: Supply Chain Attack – Masquerading

In an engagement in 2023, I was contacted by a client who was a victim of a well-targeted supply chain attack, leveraging social engineering tactics. This attack leveraged a masqueraded organization (what we call domain spoofing) as well as the compromise of a number of user mailboxes at a supplier company who provided services for this organization.

This particular organization is in the engineering space; they had most of the technology pillars covered as well as had a good handle on IT processes and were ISO 27001 compliant.

One day, a user in their finance team received an email from a Perth-based company that this organization had engaged a number of months earlier to complete a large piece of work associated with the building of a new plant for this organization. This particular company and the finance contact were frequently in touch in the past regarding payments, so when an email arrived to the usual payment person in finance, advising of a change in payment details for the latest invoice they had sent days earlier, it did not seem suspicious to the organization.

The user looked at the domain name the email was from. It looked fine, and the invoice they had re-sent was apparently a "reissued invoice," but everything in it tied up exactly to the previous invoice sent through a few days earlier; all seemed okay. The supplier (attacker) also advised that they had a new payment website that could also be used (if they didn't want to pay via bsb/acc anymore) with a URL that looked very similar to the legitimate URL, with only one extra letter in the name different, it was *redacted*constructionn.com (notice the extra n). They visited the website; it looked legit. The organization made the payment to the new account details; the amount was around $175,000.

On the supplier's end (the building company), they hadn't done their due diligence, and a user's mailbox was compromised (it didn't have MFA), nor did they have sufficient detection mechanisms. The attacker had searched through the mailbox, found recent invoices, and then re-sent them through to organizations with different details. At the same time, they cloned the organization's branding and website and set up a new website and domain. A rule was set up in the mailbox to forward all replies to the email to another folder, which the user would not see, to avoid detection. The engineering organization had also not performed sufficient vetting of the supplier (the builder in this instance), where they may have picked up the missing security controls on their end and the risks therein. They also did not have processes in place for the finance team to validate payments. All of these things combined created the perfect storm for this successful cyberattack.

Once the money hit the Australian account of the hacker (known as a mule account), it was immediately sent offshore. When both organizations had realized what had happened, the bank was only able to claw back ~30% of the money ($50k), with the rest withdrawn.

7.3.7 How Do I Vet My Suppliers or Potential Suppliers?

The best method is to provide a set of questions to each vendor to assess their cybersecurity capabilities, posture, and resilience and to assess any potential data exposure risks to your organization. The responses ideally would be reviewed by an external or independent party with a security specialization, but they can be assessed internally by people with the required skill set.

Here is a list of sample questions that I typically ask suppliers when vetting their security:

General Security Practices

- Do you have documented cybersecurity policy and procedures?

- Is your organization and/or your proposed solution compliant with any industry-recognized standards and certifications (e.g., ISO 27001, PCI, NIST, CSM, SOC2, GDPR, etc.)? Please list and send through a copy of the certificate for each certification you hold.

- How do you conduct security risk assessments of your systems and services?

- Do you perform regular vulnerability scanning and analysis of your infrastructure and systems including the infrastructure hosting the platform? How often?

- What controls do you have in place to prevent unauthorized access to data?

- Describe the security measures you have implemented to ensure a strong security posture. For example, NGFW's intrusion detection and prevention technologies, a SOC, application whitelisting, etc.

- How do you encrypt data at rest and in transit? Describe.

- How do you patch and update your systems and software?

- How do you handle security incidents? Do you have an incident response plan?

- How do you train your employees on cybersecurity awareness? If so, what is the frequency?

- Do your employees undertake regular phishing simulations? If so, what is the frequency?

- Do you conduct regular security audits and penetration testing? Please describe the schedule and provide any applicable proof of pentest certificate, report, or attestation document from the vendor.

- Do you utilize a security operations center (SOC) or a managed security provider (third party) to provide overwatch over your environment and respond to incidents? If yes, is the coverage 24 × 7/365?

- Do you utilize a Security Information and Event Management (SIEM) platform? And if so, does this incorporate Security Orchestration, Automation, and Response (SOAR) functionality?

- Are you enforcing MFA across all of your perimeter and cloud services and applied to all user accounts? Describe.

- Describe the password complexity protocols you have in place. Do you adhere to NIST recommendations for passwords, employing passphrases and banned passwords?

Incident Response and Disaster Recovery

- Do you have an internal incident response plan and processes for responding and reporting security incidents?

- How often is this tested?

- How will you notify us if there is a security incident involving our data?

- Do you have disaster recovery plans to address security incidents and recover from breaches? Describe.

Data Security

- Do you have an internal policy(ies) in place for handling sensitive data, including download, storage, and transmission?

- What type of data do you collect from us, and how is it used?

- Where will my data be stored? Will it be stored within Australia (or X location) at all times?

- Within your organization, who will have access to our data?

- What controls do you have in place to protect my data from unauthorized access or loss, such as internal threat actors, for example, disgruntled employees?

- What is your data deletion and disposal policy? What happens upon termination of our agreement?

- Do you offer any data encryption options for at-rest data and when securely transferring data to and from our organization?

Vendor Management

- Do you conduct security assessments or due diligence vetting of your own vendors and subcontractors who might access our data?

- What happens if a security breach occurs at one of your vendors?

- Do you have contractual requirements with your vendors regarding data security?

As most solution and vendor vetting is associated with SaaS and web applications, you may wish to confirm the following points:

Solution-Specific Questions for SaaS and Web Applications

- Is a web application firewall (WAF) deployed to detect and block web-based attacks? What solution is utilized?

- Does the application validate and sanitize all user input to prevent common vulnerabilities such as SQL injection and Server-Side Request Forgery (SSRF)? How?

- Is any DoS or DDoS protection in place for the application/service?

- Does the application implement comprehensive and secure logging and auditing mechanisms to detect and investigate security incidents? How?

- Does the application implement an additional layer of authentication beyond passwords (e.g., MFA, FIDO keys, etc.)?

- If yes, what methods are supported for MFA?

- Are password complexity protocols in place for the application? Are all user account passwords able to be set to be a minimum of 15 characters with a mixture of lower- and uppercase letters, numbers, and special characters?

- Are passwords in use by the end users and admins scrubbed against breached account services, such as dehashed and haveibeenpwned, to prevent users from using passwords compromised in other data breaches?

- Does the application enable centralized and secure authentication across multiple applications (i.e., single sign-on (SSO))? If yes, please also advise the SAML version supported.

- Does the application support recommended session time-outs for users for inactivity and require a captcha or additional verification for multiple login attempts?

- How many login attempts are available to users before lockout due to failed login attempts? Can this be controlled or adjusted?

- Does the application define and enforce granular administrative roles and access controls? Provide details of the admin levels and access.

- Are secure coding practices and development implemented to prevent common vulnerabilities like code injection, XSS, and CSRF?

- Does the application apply strict validation and restrictions to uploaded files to prevent malicious file uploads and extensions and ensure secure file uploads? How?

- Do uploaded files get scanned by an EDR/AV solution?

- Are third-party libraries kept up-to-date with security patches and versions? What schedule are these libraries reviewed and updated?

- Is data storage and protection in place to encrypt sensitive data at rest and in transit? Describe.

- Is role-based access control (RBAC) in place to assign privileges based on roles and least privilege principles? What?

- Are secure software development life cycle (SDLC) coding practices followed? And are regular code reviews conducted? How?

- Are mechanisms in place to anonymize sensitive/ private data stored in the web application?

- What options for secure data deletion are provided if/ when the application or any stored data is no longer used or required or the contract has terminated?

- Are IP restrictions in place to restrict access to trusted IP addresses or ranges? How?

- Are regular security audits conducted to ensure ongoing compliance with security standards and best practices? Which ones and how frequently? Are customers given the ability to review the results of the security audits?

- Do you perform regular vulnerability scanning and analysis of the infrastructure hosting the platform? How often?

- Do you perform regular penetration testing of the proposed solution and infrastructure hosting the platform? How often? And when was the last time it was performed? Please provide a copy of your latest report or proof of pentest certificate.

- If not included above, please provide the scope of testing, for example, authenticated, unauthenticated, and number of accounts.

- Is a regular data backup routine in place to ensure data availability? Provide details. Also, advise how older backups are managed and your data retention policies.

- What support pathways/contact points does the web application vendor provide to respond/investigate security-related queries from customers, and what SLAs exist around service delivery in this area?

- What documentation or training is offered by the vendor to ensure the application is used in a secure and effective manner?

- What APIs or other secure access and/or automated mechanisms are provided to integrate this system with other databases/applications (reducing the frequency of direct logins by users)?

- Are any third-party tools and integrations used by this web application? If so, how have they been vetted for security, and what data can they access?

- What data is shared with or is accessible to third parties? Describe. How have these third parties been vetted for security?

- What other security controls and features does the application provide? Please provide details.

- Does this product offer an on-premise option?

Along with the questionnaire, it is recommended to review any contracts with these suppliers and ensure they clearly outline data security expectations and responsibilities.

Consider also requesting documentation on their data security practices if available, and it is also a good idea to ask for references from other customers who can speak to their security practices.

Also, note that the preceding checklists are available via the website `https://boardroomcybersec.com/`.

This brings us to our next risk area associated with data.

7.3.8 Data

The board should be ensuring that a data inventory (as well as physical asset inventory) is performed at periodic intervals and reported to the board. Nearly all organizations are generally holding too much data, and this is a very common finding on assessments and audits that I have performed.

The first step is to understand your data:

- What data do we collect and store? This includes identifying the key types of data your organization gathers and retains.

- Who has access? Who within your organization and any external partners/supply chain have access to this data?

- Where is this data stored? What infrastructure facilitates access to this data?

- Is data storage secure and compliant? This involves ensuring data is stored securely and adheres to relevant regulations.

- Do we still need all this data? Regular data reviews are crucial to determine if all information held is still necessary.

- Data Governance Strategy: Do we have a comprehensive plan for managing data from creation to deletion?

- How is the data managed? Is it purged after a period of time or anonymized? What happens if the data is accidentally lost or deleted? What are our recovery options?

- Where are our key digital assets located? Should this be reviewed, do we have compliance or data sovereignty requirements we need to adhere to?

- What happens if we have a loss or damage to the infrastructure facilitating services and our BAU?

Also note that a basic data inventory template is available via the website: `https://boardroomcybersec.com/`.

Once you have the data inventoried, you should

1. Assess the impact if such data were to be lost or compromised.

2. Identify who has decision-making rights on access to such assets and data.

3. Identify who is responsible for the management and protection of these digital assets.

You should also ascertain what external suppliers host your data and assess how they manage access to your data, including periodic removal of old data, how they audit access to your data, and how they ensure the destruction of data at the termination of a contract (see supply chain vetting).

7.3.9 Governance of Data

Storing excessive customer and organizational data beyond legal requirements exposes both the organization and its customers to cyberattacks. This attractive target for criminals can be exploited for financial gain (such as in extortion attacks) or identity theft.

Effective data governance requires directors to grasp the volume and purpose of sensitive data held, such as personal customer and employee data. I'd encourage boards to request an annual "data map" from management, detailing the type, location, access controls, security measures, and legal justification for retaining each data set. This should also be coupled with a data purging regime based on agreed retention periods.

To minimize data risks, organizations should collect and store only the minimum personal information legally required for their services or operations and only for the minimum of time required. Often organizations continue to hold on to temporary data such as identity verification documents. It is quite common during penetration testing engagements to identify passport and driver's license scans stored within an organization's file shares, which were only needed once or twice for identity verification but were forgotten and remain stored.

This also extends to secure destruction of data. When a system has been decommissioned or repurposed, an organization should be ensuring the secure destruction of such data and physical hardware to mitigate risks associated with legacy data access.

Encryption and strict access controls are also a key component of a data strategy to safeguard sensitive data. Regularly removing unnecessary information is a key component of a comprehensive data management strategy.

7.3.10 Real-World Example – Data

All too often I find that organizations typically store way too much data and often do not restrict access to the data that they hold. This is especially prevalent in recent data breaches such as Optus and Medibank, where the organizations had a large amount of data that should have been purged at periodic intervals and in some cases, there was no real need to keep this data at all.

About 12 months ago, I was performing a pentest for a credit collection and assistance agency. They had adopted a number of security controls but had not performed any real data inventory and cleanup in many years, evident from my findings once I had obtained an entry into their network. Their network contained a number of internal network shares as well as M365 SharePoint libraries containing sensitive data. Some of the data stored within their data locations (and accessible to any user with an account) was scanned copies of passports and drivers' licenses for both staff and customers; client contact details, such as names, addresses, DOBs, tax file numbers, family information, and their contact details; the data seemed to be endless. Even in the photocopier shares were remnants of scanned documents containing PII. I even located restored data from IT where they had left files in a location after data was restored from a backup but not deleted, providing me access to backups of all of their databases and information within.

I recall most of the data was in fact stored in image files and in Excel spreadsheets with no encryption or security controls enforced (such as password-protected workbooks) – a critical finding, with an infinite probability of harm to the affected individuals if this data was accessed or exposed (not to mention any subsequent lawsuits).

7.3.11 Mitigating Risk Associated with Process and IT Functions

Business Processes and Procedures

The easiest method to reduce the risks associated with process failures is to implement defined processes both generally and to address particular threats. Your organization may already have a process mapping system, and if not, this can be implemented. There are lots of technology solutions available to create this, or it can be developed in-house. It is worth noting as well, that a lot of compliance requirements such as ISO (9001, 45001, 14001, 27001, 31000) and HACCP (Hazard Analysis Critical Control Point) require defined processes and procedures for particular controls and functions.

You should have defined what the risks and threats are that your organization is facing based on its business operations and the services you provide to customers. For example, your risk profile if you are, say, a hairdresser vs. an insurance provider would be much different. This threat and risk mapping would be created in conjunction with cyber threat intelligence, meeting with department heads and managers and analyzing existing processes and functions.

You can think of the creation of processes as the creation of flowcharts for business functions. There are lots of approaches an organization can take to process map; they can use a standard flowchart format, with standard yes–no guidance, or it can be as simple as a high-level map.

Creating a process is basically made up of these steps:

- Identify a risk/problem or process to map.

- Define the boundaries (where the process starts and stops).

- Determine and write out the sequence of steps.

- Draw out the process map/flowchart.

- Finalize and build into existing policies.

- Analyze and refine periodically.

For example, let's take the scenario of payment scams. It is a good practice to implement multiple layers of approvals for payment verification. So if an invoice comes to the account team, or a finance person is contacted by the apparent CEO, they should employ multiple layers of defense to confirm it is all legitimate before any money is sent. First, if they are called or emailed, call the company or staff member back (in this case let's use the CEO) on their mobile and confirm they called or requested a payment and the amount requested. Next, this should be compared to internal invoices, projects, etc., to confirm if it's a valid request in the first instance. Next is to get another finance person to oversee and agree to this before making the payment (this is often a line manager) to ensure complete due diligence. This layered approach provides a little extra overhead but ensures that transactions are authorized. This of course is backed up with other methods after the fact, for example, cyber insurance, backups, technical controls, etc., which we will discuss further in separate sections.

And in terms of a simple payment business process, it would look like this:

Threat: Avoiding CEO Fraud / Payment Scams
**Risk: Unauthorised payments, financial losses, image
reputation**

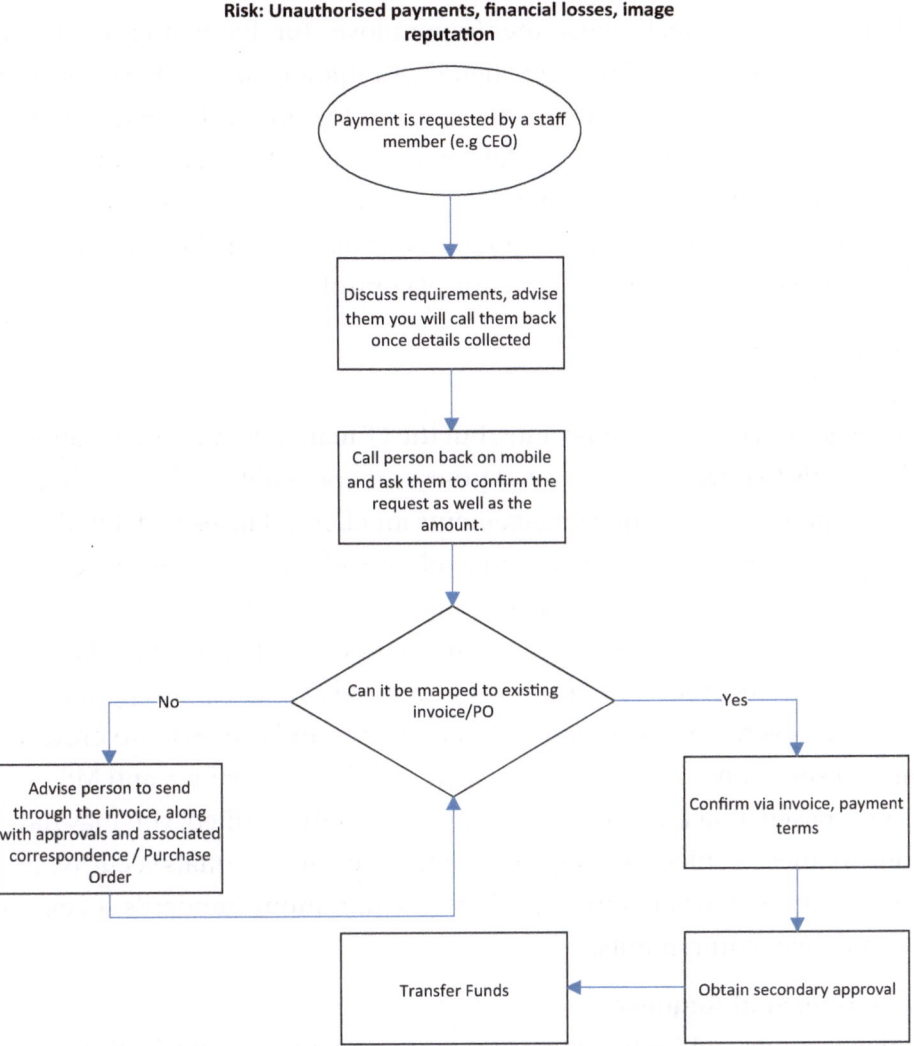

Another example is if you are customer facing and provide a service where customers will often contact you by phone to make account changes. This could lead to attacks via social engineering and vishing attacks. In this case, the organization should create a process and procedure to ensure that they have performed sufficient verification of customer queries and to not provide certain pieces of information over the phone. For example, if a customer (or employee for that matter) contacts a staff member to "confirm some details" or update details, no verification of their information should be provided over the phone; instead, get the customer to confirm via a code delivered via an SMS, email, or another form of verification to confirm they are who they say they are.

These processes then get supported by policies, which are then supported by frameworks and technical controls.

IT Processes

Business processes are important, but the IT team for your organization also needs to have a specific set of processes applicable to them. Often during penetration testing engagements for clients, lapses in defined processes have provided me a path to obtain administrator access over the whole network and access to all the organization's data.

IT teams need to have a defined set of processes to prevent risks from hygiene-related issues, such as legacy accounts, breach of test accounts, attackers leveraging too much user access, etc., and processes to protect against social engineering attacks, such as phishing, vishing, and MS teams–based attacks. If you are already ISO 27001 certified, you may have some of these in place already, but compliance never equals security, so it's recommended you aim to be above the minimum standards set out by compliance requirements.

Actioning Staff Requests

When it comes to IT, a lot of teams are underresourced, and for them, it's about closing off jobs as soon as possible and moving on to the next one. Common attack techniques I often use are calling up the helpdesk or emailing them asking to reset a password or to perform another action on the user account, such as resetting MFA, with a large degree of success. It's important that IT teams put in place a process to verify the identity of the user before actioning requests. I have seen some environments where certain requests have to go through their manager and others where they have a web portal to manage certain requests (e.g., ADManager Plus), but a new method being adopted by organizations over the last few years is performing quite well, and as such, I'll recommend it here. In this method, an employee is assigned a unique verification number (could be an employee number or a support code) that only that employee knows, and IT will not action any requests without the number. It obviously relies on the employee keeping this information anonymous and not saving it in any locations where it can be exposed. No code, no support, it's simple but effective. At the end of the day, it's up to each organization how they will verify their users, but verifying is a key component in preventing a number of attacks and lateral movement avenues.

Onboarding/Offboarding

Other recommended processes include having a complete process for onboarding and offboarding staff. It's common to find that IT teams will sometimes miss certain steps, or not have them defined; for example, they disable a user's Active Directory account but forget to remove their separate VPN account, in turn leading to access to the VPN even though everything else is disabled. It's important to have a checklist that must be followed for all on and offboarding.

Similarly, it's a common practice for IT teams to leave accounts expired or disabled for sometimes years within their environment. Even recently on an engagement, I found a disabled account (using a weak/legacy password) going back to 1999! Which could then be easily re-enabled by an attacker or adversary.

These are some examples of simple procedural and process gaps that can have massively damaging consequences.

Too Much Access and Test Machines/Accounts

Another common finding is elevated access within the IT environment. It's very common to find everyday accounts as members of the Domain Admins and Enterprise Admins groups, allowing unvetted access to the IT environment if the accounts are compromised, as well as service accounts with the same level of access (unnecessary) and granting too much access to everyday users, for example, allowing normal users to be administrators on their devices.

IT teams need to also ensure that they are only assigning the minimum amount of rights necessary for the person or account to complete their function/role and ensure they have processes in place to periodically vet and remove access to nonessential permissions.

When troubleshooting issues or completing support requests, these practices may make things easier for the IT person in the short term, but the access is often forgotten about, and these bad security practices can be absolutely detrimental to the organization in the event of a breach.

Another common practice is for IT teams to create test accounts and workstations for troubleshooting, which typically have weak passwords and are often forgotten about, again a procedure missing to clean up these accounts, but these accounts have led me to admin access in the past on many engagements.

Third-Party Access Accounts

Remember when we discussed supply chain vetting?, equally important as the initial vetting is that once a supplier has been set up, it's important to periodically review their access and periodically vet the organizations' security to ensure that their particular security posture has not changed. Often, I encounter third-party accounts with too much access and that are legacy and have been forgotten about once a third-party agreement has been terminated.

Minimum Process and Procedure Guidelines

So, putting compliance to the side, this is the minimum set of policies and procedures I would recommend you have in place. It's not exhaustive, and every organization has a unique risk profile and a unique cyber risk profile, so it should be benchmarked against services and current operational requirements – it's not a one size fits all either and should be treated as a guide.

If I had to put together a basic list of procedures and processes for your IT manager, it would look like so:

- Onboarding and offboarding processes

- Auto disablement of stale accounts

- Period reviews of admin accounts and admin memberships

- Periodic review of guest accounts locally and in M365/ cloud services

- Periodic review of standard accounts rights and test accounts

- Review of group membership changes for privileged groups

- Periodic data review processes (to be discussed in the next section)

- Payment verification processes

- User change verification processes (think permissions change)

- User management/support verification process

- Third-party review/supply chain (and initial vetting) processes

- Periodic account cleanup procedures

- Physical access procedures and processes

- Customer verification processes

- High-risk user review procedure

- Endpoint detection procedure

- Periodic firewall access list review processes

- Change management procedures

- Weekly threat review processes (What new attacks and vulnerabilities are out?)

Service Account Management and Blocking Access to Shared Mailboxes

Service accounts are essential for running various applications and services, but if not managed properly, they can pose significant security risks. Common findings associated with service accounts include:

Overprivileged Access: Service accounts often require elevated permissions to function correctly, or IT staff grant a basic service account membership like Domain Admins. If compromised, attackers can leverage these privileges to move laterally within the network and gain access to sensitive data or systems. Where possible, use Group Managed Service Accounts (GMSAs), or restrict the access and functions of service accounts.

Lack of Strong Passwords and Multi-factor Authentication (MFA): Service accounts are frequently created with weak passwords or left without MFA protection. This makes them easy targets for brute-force attacks or credential theft.

Unused or Orphaned Accounts: Organizations often have numerous service accounts that are no longer actively used. These "orphaned" accounts can be exploited by attackers who discover them.

Low Visibility and Monitoring: Service account activity often goes unnoticed by security teams. This lack of visibility makes it difficult to detect suspicious activity or identify compromised accounts.

Kerberoasting Attacks: Attackers can exploit a vulnerability called "Kerberoasting" to steal passwords associated with service accounts. This can be used to gain further access within the network.

It is a good practice to periodically review service accounts, the level of access granted to the account and the systems/data that they can access.

Additionally, another issue I commonly find is misconfiguration within mailboxes. Shared mailboxes should not be able to be logged into directly. Shared mailboxes typically lack features like strong password requirements, multi-factor authentication (MFA), or encryption capabilities, making them more vulnerable to attacks and compromise, providing an attacker access to that data.

Systems Maintenance and Housekeeping

Vulnerability Management and Patching

Another common area of risk is vulnerability management and patching. Vulnerability management is a key component of due diligence (we will discuss this extensively later in the chapter). As you are no doubt aware, new vulnerabilities are disclosed every day, and there are a number of good resources that organizations should be following to stay abreast of current risks and threats, such as

- ACSC advisories

- Vendor advisories

- SANS

- The Hacker News and BleepingComputer

- AISA

- Various threat intelligence feeds

In between these advisories and scheduled patch periods, the organization should be employing a vulnerability scanner to detect any potential vulnerabilities and vulnerable security configurations within the internal networks, before they can be exploited.

Your IT team should be consistently staying abreast of the latest advisories and performing out-of-band and scheduled patching based on advisories. The patch management process should encompass:

- **Operating Systems:** Windows, Linux, etc.

- **Hypervisors:** VMWare, etc.

- **Client-Side Applications:** Office, Adobe products, Java, any user applications

- **Firmware:** Access points, firewalls, switches, IoT devices, etc.

It is also recommended that organizations create and maintain an inventory of all assets and software to allow faster remediation of vulnerabilities and to allow more efficient patch management processes.

Patch management cycles differ from organization to organization, but a general rule of thumb is as follows:

- **Critical Vulnerabilities:** ASAP

- **High Vulnerabilities:** Within a week

- **Medium Vulnerabilities:** Within two to three weeks

- **Low-Rated Vulnerabilities:** Four to five weeks

Backups

I could easily devote a whole chapter to backups, but to simplify, you should ensure that your organization has thorough, documented, and tested backup and recovery procedures. This includes both on-site and off-site backups with defined RTO (return to operation) and RPO objectives. A DR (disaster recovery) exercise should be conducted at a minimum of annually. Backups form a key component of an organization's cyber resiliency. It is also common to find various ransomware strains that will actually go after backups, so it's important that organizations limit the number of accounts that can interact with the backups, ensure the principle of least privilege is enforced, and that off-site (and off-network) backups are maintained.

The IT manager should be reporting to the board only on the results of annual disaster recovery (DR) testing and lessons learned, to provide the board comfort in the organization's ability to respond to disaster and cyber-related events where restoration and/or contingency is required.

Housekeeping Practices That Increase Risk

It is common to find "housekeeping" vulnerabilities within internal networks that expose an organization to risk, and most often, these stem from internal IT hygiene-related issues. These include default configuration, which is where devices or systems are set up within an organization's network that are utilizing the manufacturer's default or hard-coded login details.

It is also very typical for vendors to supply and install, for example, copiers, but leave all defaults enabled, which exposes these devices to compromise.

Other IT hygiene issues I commonly encounter include information leakage, such as sensitive information exposed in account fields; this is an example from a recent penetration testing engagement:

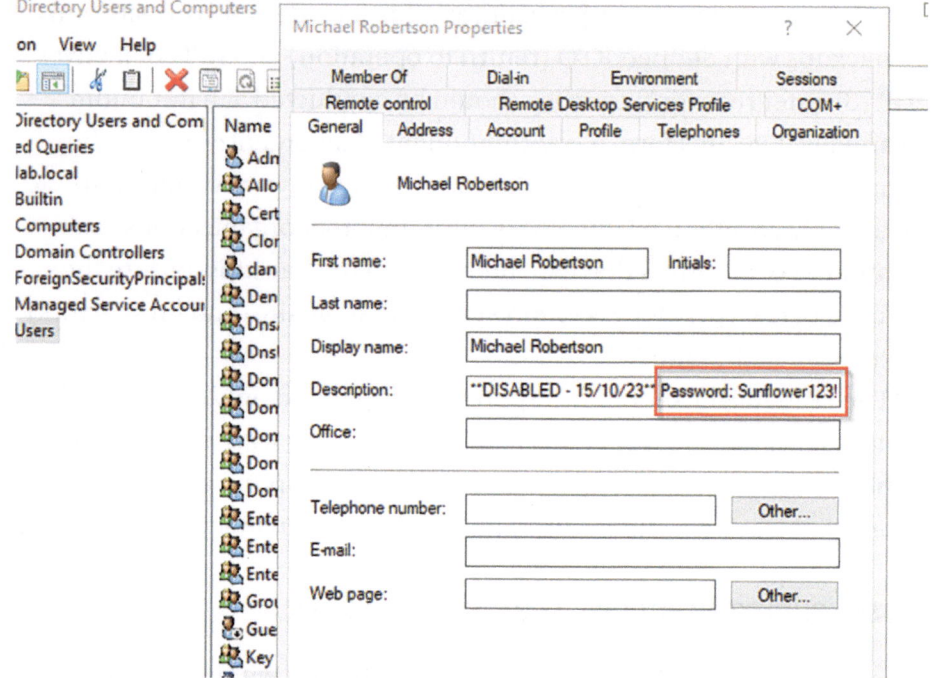

Other common hygiene-related issues I see on engagements include passwords stored in file shares and internal network drives, which provide administrative access to systems and greatly increase the risk profile from malicious insider attacks or from an external breach.

These are some examples of common housekeeping issues that are easily resolved via IT processes, periodic reviews, and procedures.

Data Governance and Missing Cleanup Practices

As mentioned previously, data governance is a large risk to most organizations. It is recommended that organizations are periodically performing a data inventory, identifying what type of data is stored, why it is stored, and the associated assets and implementing controls associated with that data.

Another often missing process and procedure is the periodic review and cleanup of data by IT within the network. It is common to find scanned drivers' licenses, passports, sensitive information such as customer data and passwords, and even medical data stored within internal network/data shares.

At periodic intervals, IT teams should be performing a review of all data stored within network drives and cloud locations such as SharePoint and OneDrive, determining what data is needed and why and archiving off any other data (or better yet, removing) and also scanning these locations for sensitive information such as passwords. Any sensitive information such as passwords should be migrated to the organization's password manager with appropriate controls applied.

Additionally, periodic access reviews should be performed to ensure that the principle of least privilege is enforced and that only the required people have access to the data. It is also a good practice to foster a culture of data hygiene within the organization, educating users to think, "do I really need to keep this data, will anyone else need this moving forward" and apply the same principles to email to ensure that only the minimum necessary data is being held within data locations and mailboxes. (It is commonplace to find a ton of sensitive data stored within user mailboxes.)

On the same token, for the data that you must keep, ensure that the data is encrypted and/or anonymized when stored, to prevent unauthorized access and disclosure, and that backups are in place.

There are also technology solutions that can assist here, such as data classification policies (the identification and tagging of files holding sensitive data) and data loss prevention (DLP) policies to limit what information can be stored and shared. We will discuss these further under the technology category.

Resources

We will discuss this further within the "Response and Visibility" section, but it's worth noting here that if your IT teams are not sufficiently funded and staffed, then these lapses in process and IT functions will continue to happen, as IT resources will prioritize day-to-day operations over hygiene and security, thus increasing the organization's overall cyber risk profile.

7.3.12 Key Questions for Your Organization

- Are there defined processes for handling sensitive information, financial transactions, and incident reporting?

- Are these processes regularly reviewed and updated to ensure they remain effective and aligned with best practices?

- Are there documented procedures for onboarding/ offboarding employees, managing user accounts (including service accounts), and handling security incidents?

- Are service accounts properly managed and secured?

- Is there a process for regular vulnerability scanning and patching of systems and software?

- Are data backups performed regularly and tested for recovery?

- Are third-party vendors and suppliers assessed for their cybersecurity practices before onboarding or contract establishment and periodically thereafter?

- Are there contractual requirements in place with vendors regarding data security and incident response?

7.4 Technology

The next pillar of cyber risk and resilience is the Technology pillar. This encompasses a larger part than most other pillars, as cyber risk in general is a technology risk, unlike fire, flood, legal, and reputational risks. Technology will form the backbone of your cyber defense strategy and will arguably require the most investment/capital. It is also common for directors to not understand these technologies in detail, which is fine, as your IT manager/security person will be responsible for understanding, implementing, and managing, but it is recommended that directors have a minimum understanding of the basic technologies that all organizations should be adopting and where required capital may need to be allocated.

You will also notice that a lot of these technological controls are closely aligned with the Essential Eight framework that we discussed previously.

The Technology area consists of four attack vectors and seven standard mitigation controls, with technologies required from two frameworks:

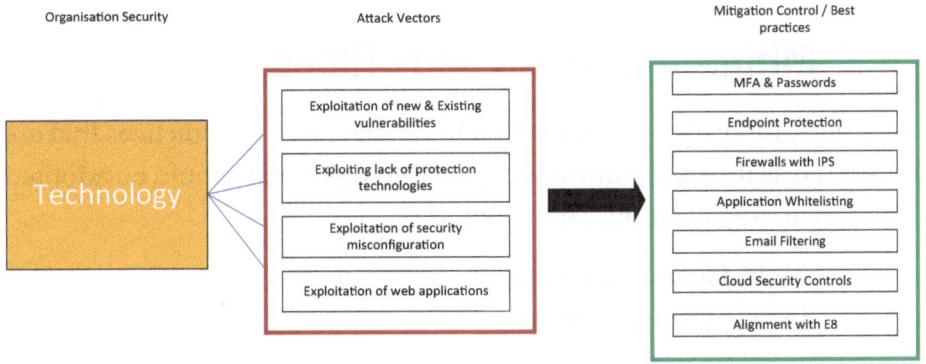

7.4.1 Attack Vectors Targeting Technology

Attack vectors targeting technology include the exploitation of newly disclosed vulnerabilities (zero-day attacks) and the exploitation of existing vulnerabilities disclosed. They make use of publicly available exploits (an exploit is a piece of malicious code designed to exploit a vulnerability in a system), and in some cases, commercial exploits are used against organizations, which are typically utilized by state-sponsored threat actors. Attackers will also leverage a lack of standard security technologies such as missing MFA, weak passwords, and missing endpoint protection. Another common attack vector is the exploitation of misconfiguration within services, for example, default credentials or default configuration applied to systems, and misconfiguration associated with the exposure of unnecessary services to the Internet, which can then be attacked, for example, remote desktop access.

Another common method is the exploiting of web application vulnerabilities, which are introduced during the development cycle or through various integrations. Attackers are relying on the presence of these vulnerabilities, as well as relying on there being no web application firewall (WAF) or other protective technology restricting attacks against the web application.

7.4.2 Mitigating Technology Risks

These days, there are a number of technologies and best practices that are considered as the minimum security technologies that should be adopted to protect an organization. These include

- Multi-factor authentication (MFA) and passwords (Now moving to Passkeys)

- Endpoint detection/protection (EDR/XDR)

- Network protections, such as next-gen firewall(s) with IPS

- Email and web filtering

- Application whitelisting

- Cloud security controls

These should be implemented along with adopting the necessary technologies associated with frameworks (discussed previously), such as the Essential Eight and alignment with Zero Trust.

There are a myriad of extra security technologies that should be adopted by organizations (the more the better), and the general rule is to implement and utilize as many as you possibly can, but in this section, I'll cover the main minimum technologies that apply to all organizations (regardless of size).

7.4.3 Multi-factor Authentication (MFA)

This is the number one most basic security technology that all organizations must adopt. If you are new to MFA, MFA is the concept of something that you know (e.g., your password) and something that you have (token, pin, or code) and something that you are (biometrics like a fingerprint or facial recognition). MFA basically stops password attacks and attacks against your accounts and provides an additional layer of protection, as an attacker would need both your password and MFA code to access your account. Every service out there offers this, and it should be enabled both on your personal accounts and all work accounts.

Password sprays are a common tactic that is employed by attackers to breach organizations, and I have breached countless organizations using this tactic. Password spraying is the process of an attacker trying one password against a large number of accounts. All the accounts are sprayed with a password (let's say Password1), then the attacker will wait for a period, then spray all accounts with Password2, then Password3, etc. These attacks typically fly under the radar for organizations as the attackers are not locking out accounts with a large number of requests (like traditional brute-force attacks), which is why these attacks continue to be successful year after year. When MFA is employed, it mitigates the risks associated with these types of attacks, because even if the attacker now has credentials, they can't access services or data as they don't have the code (unless the user hands it out or the organization is using non-MFA-supported protocols such as IMAP (Internet Message Access Protocol)).

If you are an IT person or IT manager, I know what you must be thinking... hey, we have Azure smart lockout on M365 (or Google Workspace APP); won't these technologies stop this? The answer is yes and no. Yes, these technologies will detect password sprays and prevent these sprays from continuing until the accounts are locked out; however, typically, I can get anywhere from eight to ten successful sprays (many more for on-premise services) against most services before these technologies engage, and even if they do, I find that it often still tells me when an account is valid (once smart lockout detects), but it then generates a high-risk user alert instead, but I still have the access obtained.

It is common to find that most organizations may adopt this technology with cloud services, such as Microsoft 365 or G-Suite, but very often, I find this is not enabled or enforced on the on-premise systems such as VPNs and remote desktop services (such as RDWeb), allowing attackers to successfully spray these and other services, find a valid set of credentials, and then use the concept of credential stuffing (trying an account credential against different services) to log into on-premise systems.

It is imperative that organizations ensure that MFA has been applied to *all* Internet-facing and cloud systems and MFA should also be rolled out to all user accounts. It is also very common during penetration tests to find that organizations have MFA rolled out, but a small number of accounts are excluded, and these are the accounts I usually breach in with. The only exception to this is one or two emergency "break-glass" accounts that should not have MFA and would only be used in an emergency, and these accounts would utilize super complex and long passwords as well as other safeguards.

7.4.4 Passwords

The next biggest technology risk I find across most organizations is passwords, and these directly correlate with risks associated with password sprays and breaching of non-MFA-enabled services. Passwords have been around since the dawn of technology, and in the early days, passwords were simple, like "password." Then from the old days and early versions of Windows, until only a few years back, organizations were adopting what we call standard "password complexity requirements," with a requirement for a number (and sometimes a symbol) and enforcement of typically between seven and nine characters. Then there was password expiration, which was applied on top; for example, all users need to change their password every 90 days or two or six months.

Things have changed considerably over the last few years with respect to passwords, and unfortunately, a large number of organizations are still living in the past, so to speak, and are utilizing legacy configurations. Where the risk comes in here is the type of passwords used. Utilizing these requirements, I can still have a password like Password1 or Pasw0rd!, I'm meeting the minimum characters, I have a number, but this is super easy to guess for attackers. The other challenge is that humans are predictable and like to keep things simple, so forcing users to change passwords frequently results in consecutive numbers or patterns like Password1, Password2, etc., equally just as high risk.

To that end, the new best practice (and what is recommended in the new NIST guidelines [30]) is the adoption of passphrases, which is a group of words separated by spaces and would encompass a minimum of 12 or 15+ character passwords; numbers and special characters are optional for passphrases. I recommend to organizations that they ask their users to choose four to six words that mean something to them, separated by spaces, for example:

my dogs name is ralph

Apply some basic complexity;

My dog's name is ralph!

And that's their password, complex enough, long enough (23 characters), near impossible to guess or crack from an attacker's perspective (unless the user hands it out unknowingly), and super easy for them to remember.

Then if the organization has employed MFA everywhere (or is a cloud-only organization with MFA), the password change policy can be relaxed to biannually or annually. There are so many benefits here from a security front, and users love this approach in the long term; as they don't need to change their passwords so often, it makes their lives easier and simpler.

Now for the important caveat, all organizations can and should adopt passphrases; however, if they do not have MFA employed on all of their Internet-facing and cloud services, then they *must* still utilize password change policies every month, three months, etc., as the risk profile is infinitely higher.

Then we also have a banned password list [31], which all organizations should adopt. Essentially, it's a list of words that users are not allowed to use in their password. If you are utilizing MFA and passphrases, your list may just encompass the company name as a banned password, but for organizations that are not yet ready to move to passphrases and are still utilizing legacy password standards, you should add the following to a banned password list and enforce on all users; block:

- Days of the week

- Months of the year

- Seasons

- Current or future year

- Passwords with password or welcome

- Keyboard combinations, qwerty, asdfg, etc.

- Sporting teams, football, soccer, etc.

- Functions relating to the business or business names or addresses/locations

All of these are easily guessable; for some reason, people seem to think that for us as attackers, we don't know about these types of passwords. Well, I can assure you, we definitely do.

Passkeys

Passkeys are a new authentication method that replaces traditional passwords with a more secure system. Instead of remembering complex strings of characters, users rely on their biometric data (like fingerprints or facial recognition) or a trusted device (like a smartphone) to verify their identity.

What makes passkeys more secure than passwords?

- **No Need to Remember Complex Passwords:** Passkeys eliminate the risk of forgetting or misremembering passwords, making it harder for attackers to gain access.

- **Stronger Against Phishing Attacks:** Passkeys are less susceptible to phishing attacks, as they are tied to specific devices and cannot be easily stolen or shared.

- **Enhanced Security with Biometric Data:** Using biometric data adds an extra layer of protection; as it's unique to each individual and they need to physically be you, it's very difficult to replicate.

- **Simplified Login Process:** Passkeys offer a more seamless login experience, reducing the friction associated with traditional password-based authentication.

7.4.5 Password Manager

Password management and secure storage of passwords is another high-risk area for a number of organizations. I frequently locate passwords stored in text files, mailboxes, and file shares when performing penetration testing for clients. The easiest and simplest way to mitigate this risk is to adopt a password manager. A password manager is a central point where you store all of your organization's passwords, and then the users only need to remember one master password (or use single sign-on (SSO)) to access the password manager. MFA can then be enforced on the password manager. There are a number of local on-premise and cloud-based products, and choosing a password manager is dependent on your use case. For example, if you wish to have an on-prem solution, then remote users would require a VPN connection to access the password manager, or if you would like to adopt a cloud-based solution to ensure that access is always available to passwords. It is worth noting that a lot of the cloud-based password managers for business do allow restricting access by IP addresses so that you can still enforce, say, a VPN connection before accessing the manager.

Password managers should also be promoted across the organization to ensure that staff are utilizing these for their personal accounts and building good password storage best practices.

7.4.6 Endpoint Protection

The next technology control is endpoint protection (what used to be termed antivirus in the old days). These days, there are two types of endpoint protection: EDR and XDR. EDR and XDR operate very similarly, in that they allow for detection and response to local endpoint attacks; however, they differ in their scope and capabilities:

EDR (endpoint detection and response) is focused on protecting endpoints such as laptops, desktops, servers, and mobile devices. It provides detailed visibility and threat protection for these individual devices. EDR typically collects data only from endpoints, including logs, events, and telemetry data generated by endpoint security tools. It then uses this endpoint data to identify suspicious activity that might indicate a cyberattack. This could include unusual file access patterns, malware execution attempts, or unauthorized network connections.

EDR performs your standard response actions, such as isolating an infected device, blocking malicious traffic, or initiating a remediation process.

XDR (extended detection and response), on the other hand, takes a broader view of security, extending beyond endpoints to encompass your entire security ecosystem. This can include network security devices, cloud services, email security solutions, and identity and access management (IAM) systems. It is common to see XDR most of the time these days, as these products are often leveraged by SOCs (security operation centers) to provide visibility into endpoint attacks and provide telemetry data to then be acted upon.

XDR collects and aggregates data from multiple sources, providing a more holistic view of potential threats and allowing for better correlation of events across different parts of your security infrastructure. It also has better detection abilities; XDR can detect more sophisticated attacks that might involve multiple systems or stages. It can also identify complex threat patterns and anomalies that might be missed by EDR alone.

XDR provides similar response capabilities as EDR but with the advantage of a more comprehensive view of the attack, allowing for a more coordinated and effective response strategy.

Let's use the house again as an example:

EDR is like having a security guard at each door of your house. They can monitor activity and raise an alarm if they see something suspicious.

XDR is like having a central security system with cameras and sensors throughout your house. It can not only monitor individual doors but also correlate activity across different areas to identify a break-in attempt in progress.

7.4.7 Next-Gen Firewalls (NGFW)

Everyone is pretty across firewalls these days as they have been around since the dawn of interconnected devices. Every organization will have one to facilitate Internet connectivity, to protect their assets, and to control inbound and outbound network traffic that is allowed. The main point I wanted to get across here is that not all firewalls are equal just like not all coffee beans are equal. These days, we have what's called next-generation (next-gen) firewalls or NGFWs. They provide the standard functionality as existing firewalls, including facilitating VPN access to your networks, but current next-gen firewalls offer a range of security enhancements and capabilities over older firewalls, such as:

> **Web Filtering:** Newer firewalls provide the ability to apply limits and restrictions on web traffic and browsing for the end users. In the past, this was accomplished through separate systems connected to your networks or agents installed on all machines, but these days, it's built into the firewall, allowing you to restrict dangerous web traffic and user behaviors as well as enforce policies on the users.
>
> NGFWs can also block access to malicious or inappropriate websites based on predefined categories or blacklists.
>
> **Deep Packet Inspection (DPI):** Unlike traditional firewalls that only inspect packet headers, NGFWs use what we call DPI (or SSL inspection) to examine the actual content of data packets. This allows them to identify malware, connections to malicious command and control (C2) servers, application vulnerabilities, and other threats hidden within traffic.

Application Awareness and Control: NGFWs can recognize different types of applications like web browsing, email, or videoconferencing as well as network protocols. This enables them to control and filter traffic based on specific applications, allowing you to prioritize critical business applications and traffic (what we call QoS, or Quality of Service) and blocking unauthorized apps and traffic.

Intrusion Prevention System (IPS): IPS and IDS (intrusion detection system) functionality is now integrated within the firewall, which actively searches for and blocks malicious network activity such as denial-of-service attacks, port scans, and exploit attempts.

Threat Intelligence: NGFWs can leverage threat intelligence feeds to stay updated on the latest vulnerabilities and malicious tactics. This allows them to proactively block known threats and suspicious activities.

Sandboxing: Some NGFWs offer sandboxing, which creates a secure isolated environment to detonate suspicious files or URLs. By analyzing the file's behavior in the sandbox, the NGFW can identify and block malware before it can infect the network.

Application Security Features: Some NGFWs offer additional application security features like data loss prevention (DLP) and web application firewalls (WAF) to further tighten security against application-layer attacks.

Firewalls should be replaced as soon as they are no longer supported and update the firewall(s) frequently to ensure that they are operating efficiently and effectively.

7.4.8 Application Whitelisting

Another key technology that is also flagged in the Essential Eight is the adoption of application whitelisting. Application whitelisting is a security technology and method that enforces strict control over what software can run on a device. By creating a preapproved list of authorized applications, only those programs are allowed to execute.

This approach significantly reduces the risk of malware infections, ransomware attacks, and attacker tooling that runs in memory on local devices and also protects against unauthorized software installations.

It essentially operates on a "deny by default" basis, blocking any unknown application unless explicitly approved by an administrator.

Application whitelisting has been around for a long time now but has seen a slow adoption across organizations due to perceived admin overhead but does significantly reduce the attack surface of user devices. Microsoft has built this into the Windows and Active Directory environment already (e.g., AppLocker), which organizations can adopt; there are also separate application whitelisting products available, and most EDR/XDR products these days incorporate some degree of application whitelisting that can be configured, so there are lots of options for deployment.

7.4.9 Email Filtering

These days, most organizations have email filtering employed to protect their user base, and mail service providers (such as M365) by default provide a base level of filtering and features.

It's important to take a layered approach to email security. Typically, this involves two layers of filtering, one through a third-party service as the first boundary and then a backup boundary on-premise or in M365/G-Suite.

Your organization should also ensure that they are utilizing a number of standard protective controls, including

- **Impersonation Filtering:** Block similar or other domains masquerading as your organization

- **Implementing Security Technologies:** For example, DKIM, SPF, and DMARC

7.4.10 USB Controls

It is recommended that all organizations implement basic security controls to restrict the use of USBs and external hard drives. USB keys and drives, while convenient for data transfer, pose several cybersecurity risks. They can be easily lost or stolen, potentially exposing sensitive information stored on them. Malicious actors can also use them to introduce malware on to a system. Infected USB drives can bypass traditional security measures and spread malware or ransomware when plugged into a device. Additionally, some USB drives may contain hidden partitions or auto-run features that can trigger malicious code without the users' knowledge. Overall, the ease of use and physical nature of USB drives make them a potential entry point for cyberattacks if proper caution is not exercised.

USBs can be restricted in many ways through technology. In the Microsoft world, this can be accomplished through what we call Group Policies, or the Device Guard technology, which forms part of the Microsoft Defender for endpoint product. For other devices (and you can use it on Microsoft devices too), there are many third-party endpoint security solutions that offer more granular control over USB access, including DLP solutions, USB blocker software, and Device Control software.

7.4.11 Cloud Security Controls

Most organizations are now partially or fully in the cloud. Cloud in general provides a reduced risk profile and a stronger security posture than on-premise infrastructure. The cloud can obviously present its own risks if not correctly configured and managed.

Here are the top six cloud security technologies that an organization should consider adopting:

Zero Trust Security: We discussed this in detail in earlier chapters, but a zero trust approach should be adopted for all cloud-connected users and devices. Recall, this model assumes no user or device is inherently trustworthy inside or outside the network. Every access attempt is verified regardless of location or origin. This can be achieved through techniques like multi-factor authentication, conditional access, and micro-segmentation of the cloud environment.

Cloud Security Posture Management (CSPM): A CSPM tool continuously monitors and assesses an organization's cloud environment for security vulnerabilities and misconfigurations. It helps ensure the cloud environment is set up securely and identifies areas for improvement.

Cloud Access Security Broker (CASB): A CASB acts as a central control point for managing access to cloud services. It enforces security policies, monitors user activity, and can prevent data breaches.

Cloud Security Automation: Automating security tasks like vulnerability scanning, patching, and incident response can improve efficiency and reduce human error.

Secret Management: This involves securing sensitive data like passwords, API keys, and encryption keys. Secret management tools can help organizations store, manage, and rotate these credentials securely.

From a vendor technology perspective, the following minimum controls should be adopted.

Microsoft 365 (M365)/Azure

Microsoft Entra ID (Formerly Azure Active Directory) (AAD) Multi-factor Authentication (MFA): Enforce MFA for all M365 logins and disable authentication and protocols that do not support MFA or that allow it to be bypassed.

Entra ID Conditional Access: Implement conditional access policies to restrict access to M365 resources based on factors like location, device type, and user risk level. For example, require MFA for access from unknown devices or high-risk locations.

Microsoft Defender for Cloud Apps (MDCA): Utilize MDCA to continuously monitor M365 activity for suspicious behavior and potential data breaches. MDCA can help detect and prevent malware, phishing attacks, and unauthorized access to sensitive data. We will discuss how a SIEM and SOC comes into play in the next pillar.

Microsoft Purview Data Loss Prevention (DLP): Implement DLP policies to prevent sensitive data from being accidentally or intentionally shared externally. DLP can scan emails, documents, and other M365 content for keywords or patterns that indicate sensitive data and block outgoing messages or files that violate DLP rules.

Cloud App Security for Microsoft 365: This service extends cloud access security broker (CASB) functionality to M365. It allows you to centrally manage access to shadow IT (unsanctioned cloud services), gain visibility into user activity, and enforce security policies across all M365 apps.

Microsoft Defender for Endpoint: This feature allows you extend security beyond M365 with a unified endpoint protection platform that detects and prevents malware, ransomware, and other threats across devices accessing M365 data.

Microsoft Intune: This feature helps organizations manage and secure all of their devices, such as desktops, laptops, and mobile devices that are connected to M365 services and access data; it lets you deploy apps, enforce security policies, and wipe lost or stolen devices.

Enable Identity Governance for M365: This feature encompasses Microsoft Entra access reviews (which allows you to review a user's access to ensure only the right people have continued access) and Entra entitlement management, which allows you to manage the identity and access life cycle by automating access request workflows, access assignments, reviews, and expiration.

Disable User Ability to Register or Consent to Apps:
There are several significant risks associated with allowing users to register or consent to apps in M365 without proper oversight.

Users might unknowingly install malicious applications that masquerade as legitimate ones. These apps could steal data, install malware, or disrupt M365 functionality. Users could register and start using unauthorized cloud services (shadow IT), which creates risks because these apps might not meet your organization's security standards or compliance requirements.

Malicious apps or those with weak security practices could expose sensitive data stored in M365, which could lead to data exposure/breaches. Also, consider wasted resources, users might register for apps they don't need or use effectively, and of course, there are integration issues or compatibility problems associated with such apps.

G-Suite (Google)

Context-Aware Access (CAA): Similar to conditional access in M365, CAA in Google Workspace allows you to set access controls based on various contextual factors. You can define policies that restrict access to Google Workspace resources (like Gmail, Drive, etc.) based on user attributes, locations, device types, application, and risk level.

Advanced Protection Program (APP): APP offers an extra layer of security for Google Workspace accounts. It enforces stricter authentication methods like mandatory security keys for logins and restricts access from unknown devices or locations. This adds an additional security barrier on top of CAA policies.

Security Keys and MFA: Similar to M365, Google Workspace supports strong authentication methods like security keys and multi-factor authentication (MFA).

Cloud Identity Platform (CIP): CIP is Google's cloud-based identity and access management (IAM) solution. It allows you to centrally manage user access across Google Workspace and other cloud applications, simplifying administration and enhancing security.

It's important to note that in cloud environments, groups of technologies work together to provide a higher level of visibility and security; for example, M365 ties in with MFA which ties in with conditional access, with DLP policies applied to Intune-connected devices. So, where possible, if you can utilize technologies from the same vendor (rather than mixed or disparate technologies), it provides the best result.

Alignment with Essential Eight

As mentioned previously, the ACSC Essential Eight is a good starting baseline to ensure you are adopting the basic cybersecurity technologies within your organization. The technologies associated with E8 are

- Patch applications, including application patching, Windows patching, firmware patching, and vulnerability scanning

- Application whitelisting

- Restricting Microsoft Office Macros

- Multi-factor authentication (MFA)

- Restricted administrative privileges (limiting user accounts with administrative rights to minimize the potential damage from compromised accounts)

- Daily backups

- User application hardening (configuration settings that minimize vulnerabilities within applications, like disabling unnecessary features)

More information can be found on the ACSC website [32].

7.4.12 Real-World Example – Technology

Nearly every data breach out there leverages lapses in technology in one form or another. Most attacks and successful breaches of organizations are due to missing MFA and weak password adoption. If we take some very basic examples:

- **Marriott International (2018):** Hackers breached Marriott's Starwood guest reservation system due to a misconfigured firewall. The firewall wasn't set up to block access from unauthorized locations, allowing attackers to gain access to the system. Proper firewall configuration could have prevented this breach.

- **Target (2013):** This infamous breach involved attackers gaining access to Target's point-of-sale systems through a compromised vendor's credentials. While Target had firewalls in place, the malware used bypassed them, due to missing multi-factor authentication (MFA) for remote access. This additional layer of security could have prevented unauthorized access.

- **Capital One (2019):** A former Amazon Web Services (AWS) employee gained access to the personal information of over 100 million Capital One credit card applicants. The attacker exploited a misconfigured firewall rule that allowed unauthorized access to a cloud storage bucket containing the data. This breach highlights the importance of proper cloud security configurations and access controls.

- **TAFE NSW (2020):** A data breach at TAFE NSW in Australia exposed the personal information of nearly half a million students and staff. Hackers gained access through a compromised staff email account due to a lack of multi-factor authentication (MFA).

- **Colonial Pipeline (2021):** This ransomware attack targeted a major US oil pipeline operator. While the specifics are still being investigated, initial reports suggest the attackers may have gained access through a compromised VPN account that lacked strong password protocols.

As a tester, I can tell you we have two main ways to breach into any organization, social engineering (i.e., phishing, vishing, smishing, USB drops, physical access, etc.), and through missing or weak technology, such as weak passwords, missing MFA, misconfiguration of services, and exploiting of legacy systems and technology. I have compromised countless organizations (almost daily) through exploitation of vulnerabilities in systems that could have easily been prevented through regular patch management and hygiene processes and by implementing various protective technologies and controls such as MFA and password restrictions.

One of my earliest pentests that I performed (many, many years back, which I will never forget) was for a large architecture firm that had a name of three letters (let's call them ABC Architecture); they had it configured so that every single person in the organization had the same password, which never expired and never needed to be changed. Their reasoning was that they needed staff to access other users' accounts and mailboxes if they were away from the office. They also had direct remote access for staff, so people could work from home, and this remote access (what's called RDP) didn't have MFA and was wide open via a connection on the firewall. I'll let you guess what the password was that was configured for the 50 odd people who made up the organization... you guessed it, "abc." It was my fastest-ever breach at six minutes where I had my entry point into the network and access to their data and all accounts.

It is important to remember that once an attacker has an entry point (foothold), it is only a matter of time before they eventually get access to all data and systems you hold within your environment (especially if you can't detect the attack and/or haven't implemented these controls).

And more often than not, the attacker will not be detected. If we look at recent breaches, for example:

- **Medibank Private (2022–2023):** This major breach remains under investigation, but estimates suggest the attackers may have been in Medibank's system for four months before detection.

- **Optus (2022):** While the exact timeframe is unclear, reports suggest the attackers may have been present for weeks before being discovered. This extended dwell time allowed them to access a large amount of data.

- **Australian Red Cross Blood Service (2016):** This breach involved unauthorized access to the Red Cross Blood Service network for months. The attackers remained undetected while potentially accessing sensitive donor information.

7.4.13 Mitigating Risk Associated with Technology

So to mitigate technology risks, quite simply, adopt as many of the technologies as possible outlined in this section, and ensure that you have all of these covered. If you are still utilizing on-prem infrastructure, now might be a good time to assess your cloud migration strategy and plan to migrate away from on-premise infrastructure and technology, which presents an infinitely larger risk from cyberattacks, and poor internal practices can further increase this risk.

7.4.14 Key Questions for Your Organization

- Is MFA implemented for all user accounts and Internet-facing systems?

- Are there any exceptions to MFA, and if so, are they justified (e.g., break-glass accounts) and secured with alternative measures like strong passwords and additional monitoring?

- Are strong password policies in place, encouraging the use of passphrases and avoiding easily guessable passwords?

- Is there a banned password list to prevent the use of weak or compromised passwords?

- Is a password manager used to securely store and manage passwords?

- Is MFA enabled for the password manager?

- Have we implemented any controls to restrict USB usage?

- Is endpoint protection software (EDR/XDR) deployed on all devices?

- Is the endpoint protection software regularly updated and monitored for effectiveness?

- Is a next-generation firewall (NGFW) in place with features like web filtering, intrusion prevention, and deep packet inspection?

- Are network security devices regularly updated and monitored for security and performance?

- Are email and web filtering solutions in place to block malicious content and websites?

- Is application whitelisting implemented to control what software can run on devices?

- Have we applied the principle of least privilege, restricting users to only the necessary access and functions required on their devices and within our systems?

- Are appropriate security controls in place for cloud services used by the organization, such as conditional access, MFA, GEO restrictions, and cloud security posture management (CSPM)?

- Have we deployed mobile device technologies (MDM and MAM) to protect data stored on mobile devices?

- Are cloud configurations regularly reviewed for security and compliance?

7.5 Response and Visibility

This pillar is one of the most important pillars for ensuring organizational security and is often the most lacking area for most organizations. Over the last 17+ years of pentesting, there have been only a very small number or organizations that have detected my attacks during an engagement (let alone stopped them) when they were under way. We know cyberattacks and breaches are inevitable, but if you do not know an attack is under way, how can you possibly defend against it?

Response and Visibility is an absolute key when it comes to ensuring organizational cyber resilience. As a director, you (and the board in general) should be preparing and planning for a cyber incident, of which will most likely be significant. As well as planning, the organization should be adopting various technologies and processes (such as incident simulation exercises) to ensure that the organization can quickly and effectively respond to an incident (and adhere to any mandatory reporting obligations) and refine such processes, through lessons learned and refinement of incident response processes after a simulation.

The Response and Visibility area consists of five attack vectors that are often leveraged and nine standard mitigation controls:

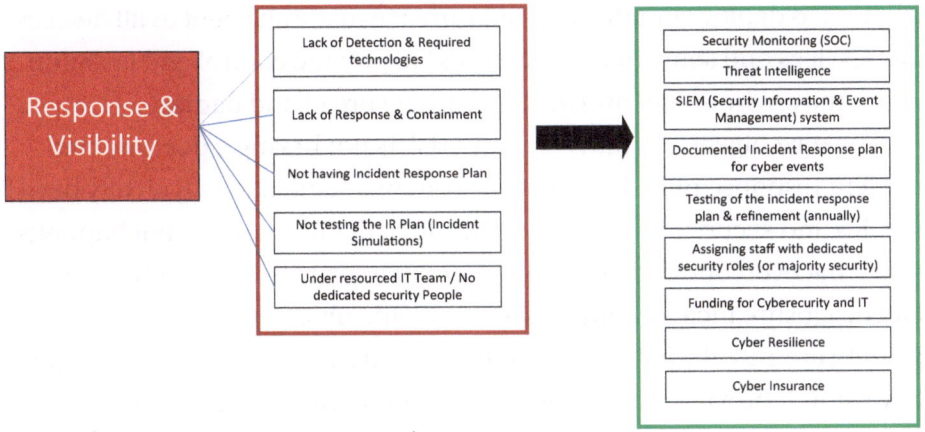

Attack Vectors Targeting Response and Visibility

If we examine the attack vectors above, threat actors will be counting on a lack of detection and visibility technologies. The longer they can stay undetected in a network, cloud, and/or user account, the more data they can exfiltrate, and the more money they can potentially extort from their victims. Along with the lack of initial detection, attackers are also leveraging a lack of response and containment measures. We see this often during penetration testing engagements and with organizations that have been breached. Usually, the breach of a service or account is detected often hours, sometimes days after the initial breach has happened (sometimes never). It's important to note that in a breach, seconds and minutes matter; the longer attackers are in, the worse it gets. If we take the Medibank [33] and Latitude [34] breaches as an example, the attackers were in the network for a substantial amount of time before detection, even an hour is a long time for customer data, PII, and other sensitive information to be in the hands of attackers.

With a lack of response and containment, attackers can continue to laterally move throughout a network as well as deploy additional backdoors for persistent access and continue propagation spreading such as malware. That is why if you are breached, the first thing the incident response firm will do is to deploy containment measures (usually an agent to all devices and services and some network devices) to provide control and isolation within the environment and to stop further spread and damage.

The next biggest threat vector and risk is not having a documented incident response plan. I see this very often; organizations typically have IT policies and security policies but nothing to define exactly what happens (and what everyone will do) in the event of a security breach incident or data disclosure incident. Attackers are relying on this too – if everyone is running around like chickens with their heads cut off, this chaos is what they want; it provides for limited containment from the attacker's end and increases the panic level within the organization, making them more likely to pay an extortion when it comes.

An incident response plan should also be tested annually to provide assurance (and refinement) of the organizations' ability to respond to cyber events (we will discuss this further shortly). The last area that attackers love to exploit is underresourced IT teams. As mentioned previously, IT often get lumped with the security hat, and as IT teams are consistently under the pump, attacks can and do often go undetected, without sufficient funding and resourcing for IT and security teams.

7.5.1 In-House Security Teams and SOCs

These days, not many organizations have on-site IT security teams. It's not to say they don't exist, but they are commonly found in the enterprise and government space, more than SMBs and midsized companies. Often IT staff might have to take on that role (or their managed service or SOC provider), or they may have someone internally that looks after security, but that person doesn't have that as their primary role and operates with more of a hybrid setup, with outsourced third parties taking on the heavy lifting. There is no right or wrong way of doing it, and it ties back to the organizations' risk appetite, budget considerations, and operating model for IT and security. If you were considering a dedicated security operations center (SOC) of your own or dedicated security resources, there will be technology-related capital expenditure as well as standard staff wages, learning and development costs, and other overheads. Often, organizations that don't want to use any third parties or have an air-gapped design or are critical infrastructure may choose to host these resources and teams in-house.

If we discuss technology capital and budgets required, such a team typically would require the following toolsets/technology:

- A SIEM (we discuss this next)

- Standard resource costs

- Subscriptions associated with threat intelligence feeds

- Dark web monitoring tools/toolsets

- Software to provide visibility and endpoint control/ isolation

- Hardware or upgrading of existing hardware (and subscriptions), for example, firewalls, to allow for additional security detection and logging

- Security appliances (such as IDS/IPS and network traffic analysis (NTA))

- Vulnerability management software and vulnerability scanning software

- Security Orchestration, Automation, and Response (SOAR) tools/subscriptions

- Security training

So there is a fair bit of outlay.

7.5.2 What the Heck Is a SIEM?

A SIEM (Security Information and Event Management) solution is basically the center of a SOC or security team. It amalgamates (takes in) data and events from firewalls, network devices, endpoints and endpoint protection, servers, IPS, cloud services, active directory, and user behavior analytics (basically everything running within an organization); then analyzes the data, categorizes the data, and makes an assessment based upon identified activities, patterns, traffic, and threats; and generates alerts for security resources or SOC personnel to review and act upon.

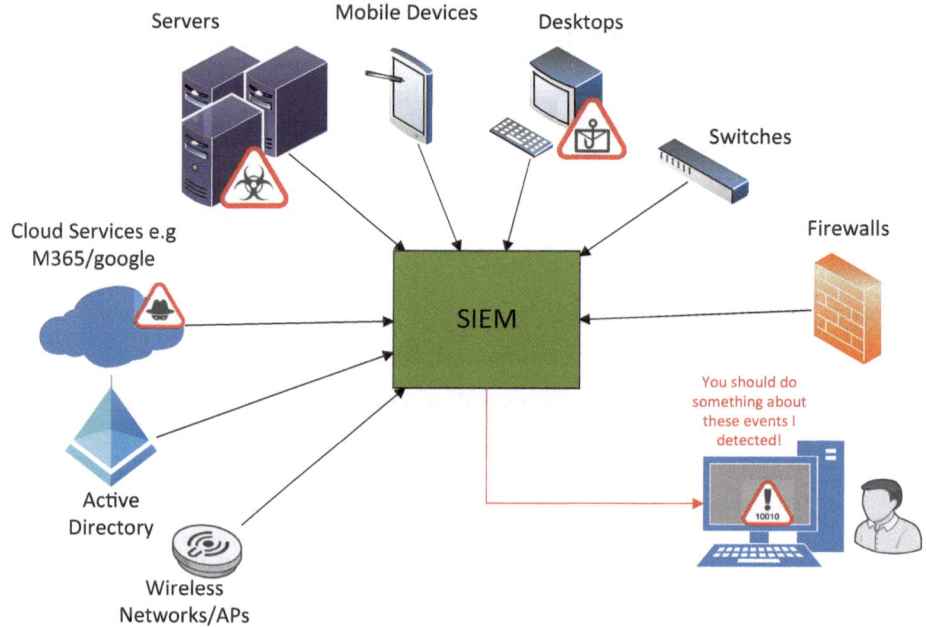

Then we have what's called SOAR (Security Orchestration, Automation, and Response), which works in tandem with a SIEM system to streamline security operations and improve incident response efficiency; it also automates routine security tasks, allowing analysts to focus on complex investigations and incident response activities. It also utilizes user and entity behavior analytics (UEBA), sometimes called end-user behavior analytics. UEBA collects data on user activities, login attempts, file access, device usage patterns, and application behavior. It then analyzes this data using machine learning algorithms to identify patterns and deviations from normal behavior. It looks like this:

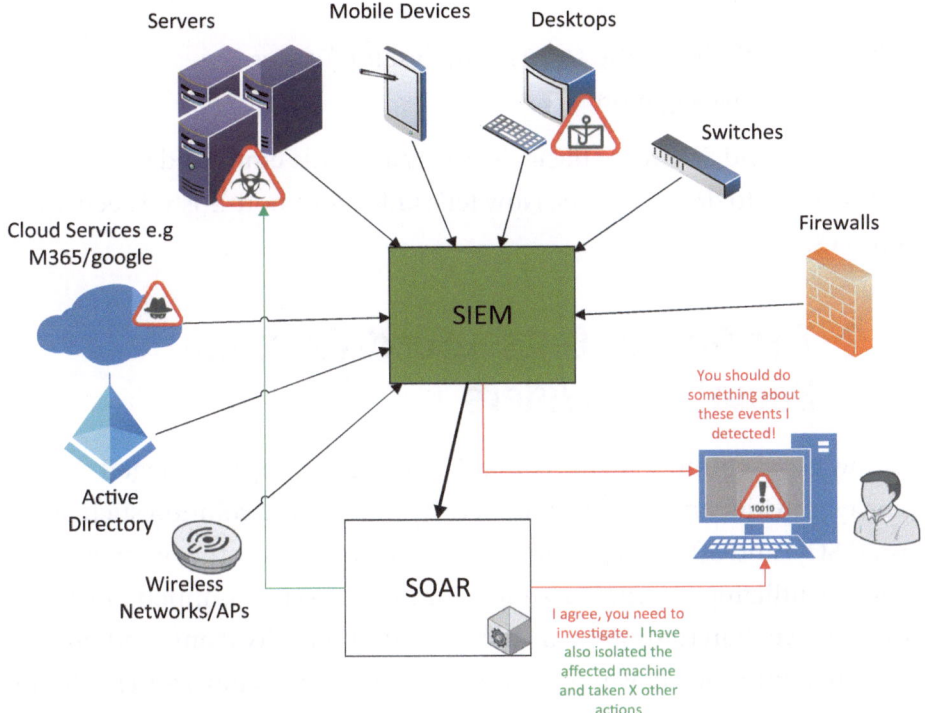

Here's an example of how SOAR and SIEM work together:

- The SIEM detects a suspicious login attempt on a user account from an unknown location.

- The SIEM sends an alert to SOAR.

- SOAR analyzes the alert and determines it might be a compromised account.

- SOAR triggers actions like

  - Blocking the login attempt.

  - Resetting the user's password.

  - Isolating the potentially compromised device from the network.

  - Notifying the security analyst for further investigation.

So SIEM and SOAR are basically the main tools employed by organizations to detect events. Now let's talk about non-hosted security resources.

7.5.3 The Role of Outsourced/External Security Providers

It is now more common to find organizations adopting a managed security provider and/or external security monitoring solution such as a hosted SOC and SIEM, to provide 24 × 7 overwatch over the organization. Typically, utilizing external providers for these services is much more cost-effective than traditional in-house hosted security teams and provides additional time zone coverage (think after-hours detection) and facilitates an immediate response to threats. There is also a point here on risk transference.

A lot of endpoint protection providers will also utilize their standard installed endpoint protection on servers and devices, to facilitate analytics to their SOC and allow for containment controls as part of one complete solution, rather than deploying additional tools/technologies, so it is very common to find organizations adopting one endpoint protection technology and wrapping this agreement with a managed SOC and SIEM agreement with the same vendor.

The security provider will also have their own threat intelligence feeds and can assist the organization with development and refining of their incident response processes, which we will discuss further in upcoming sections.

Another benefit of this arrangement is that your organization receives threat intelligence from a number of companies; for example, if we take M365's sentinel SIEM, it's cloud-based, and if one phishing campaign is seen across say 50 companies using M365, then Microsoft may push that filter to all other clients using M365, so this is where being in the cloud provides big benefits because of these extra intelligence sources and vendor activities, allowing attacks to be stopped before they even target your organization.

The same applies to managed security providers; they may see attacks targeting some of their other clients, of which they then apply the same protective/mitigation control(s) to your organization to further future-proof your organization from potential upcoming attacks.

7.5.4 Threat Intelligence

Threat intelligence is a crucial aspect of cybersecurity that involves the collection, analysis, and dissemination of information about cyber threats. It helps organizations understand the who, what, where, when, why, and how of cyberattacks, allowing them to proactively defend their systems and data. Even if you are a small business or not utilizing dedicated security resources, it is still recommended that you employ threat intelligence as part of your overall cyber resilience, with new risks and threats discussed at board meetings.

Typically, threat intelligence involves collecting data from various sources, including:

Internal Security Tools: Security logs, SIEM data, and endpoint detection and response (EDR) reports.

External Threat Feeds: Subscriptions to feeds from cybersecurity vendors (such as the ACSC), government agencies, or industry groups that provide information about known threats, indicators of compromise (IOCs), and attacker tactics, techniques, and procedures (TTPs).

Open Source Intelligence (OSINT): Publicly available information like news reports, social media discussions, and malware analysis reports by security researchers.

Dark Web Resources: Analyzing dark web postings/ information to identify references to your organization within dark web content. This would typically identify if a breach or data disclosure has occurred.

This information is then collected and analyzed to identify patterns, trends, and potential threats and then disseminated to security teams in a way that is actionable. This might involve creating reports, threat briefs, or updating security tools with the latest threat information.

There are a number of benefits associated with threat intelligence, for example, proactive defense capabilities, and by understanding current threats and attacker tactics, organizations can implement preventive measures and reduce the risk of successful cyberattacks. This may be applying firmware, patches, or configuration changes as an example.

Threat intelligence also provides improved incident response. Threat intelligence can help identify the nature and scope of an attack faster, leading to a more effective and timely response. And the last benefit is associated with better resource planning and allocation. By understanding the most likely risks and threats, organizations can prioritize their security resources and focus on areas of greatest risk.

There are a stack of resources available to organizations and individuals, including:

The Australian Cyber Security Centre (ACSC): The ACSC offers a wealth of resources on cyber threats, including threat reports, mitigation advice, and information on subscribing to their threat intelligence feeds: `www.cyber.gov.au/`.

Cybercrime and Security Research Centre (CSRC): Established by Macquarie University, the CSRC conducts research on cybercrime and cybersecurity threats relevant to Australia: `www.mq.edu.au/partner/ access-business-opportunities/innovation- entrepreneurship-and-it/cyber-security-hub`.

Australian Information Security Association (AISA): AISA is a nonprofit organization that promotes cybersecurity awareness and best practices in Australia. They offer resources and events related to cyber threats: `www.aisa.org.au/`.

Australian Signals Directorate (ASD): While the ASD is a government intelligence agency, they occasionally release unclassified threat reports that can be valuable resources: `www.asd.gov.au/`.

There are also a ton of other resources available via email, websites, and social media feeds including

- The Hacker News [35]
- BleepingComputer [36]
- SANS @Risk [37]
- The *Washington Post* – Technology 202 [38]

- Packet Storm [39]

- Microsoft Security Blog [40]

- Standard LinkedIn and Twitter feeds

By utilizing these resources and incorporating threat intelligence into your cybersecurity strategy, you can significantly enhance your organization's ability to defend against cyber threats.

7.5.5 Defining an Incident Response Plan

A lot of organizations struggle with the defining of an incident response plan for cyber events. The Cyber Security Incident Response Plan (CSIRP) should be implemented, tested annually at a minimum, and regularly updated. NIST as well as the ACSC have some amazing resources to assist with the development of an incident response plan [41][42][43].

To develop the CSIRT from a high level:

The first step is to assemble who will make up your CSIRT team. This stage is all about building a strong foundation. Form your cyber incident response team, clearly defining roles and assigning responsibilities for each member. Identify both internal resources (like IT specialists) and external partners (security firms, incident response firms, PR, etc.) who can assist during an attack. Your cyber insurance details should also make up your team members, as you may need to call on your insurance who will then put you in touch with their preferred specialists.

An organization should also assess whether the resources available to the management team are sufficient to effectively respond to this incident, considering the organization's size, complexity, and the specific nature of the cyberattack.

Additionally, to ensure agile decision-making during a cyber crisis, larger organizations should consider forming a dedicated Cyber Incident Sub-Committee within the board.

A well-defined CSIRT should outline clear roles and responsibilities for directors and the board and any associated committees and management during a cyber incident.

This plan should encompass:

Decision-Making Processes: How critical decisions will be made during a crisis. During a significant event, the board should provide timely support, oversight, and decision-making for the organization.

Communication Protocols: Strategies for internal and external communication throughout the incident.

Roles and Responsibilities: Clear delineation of roles for both the board and senior management.

Understanding Insurance Coverage: Knowing the limitations and support offered by cyber insurance policies.

This section should also define the types of incidents that will require the CSIRP to be activated and how that assessment/decision will be made.

Important Note: Often during an incident, the attack is quite destructive, such as ransomware outbreaks and purposefully taking down systems. It is strongly advisable that you maintain an offline list of who should be contacted as well as contact details, including external parties who can assist in a significant event, and which key stakeholders to communicate with. Ideally, a copy of the plan in full should be kept offline in paper form in case internal systems and data are not available during the incident and you need to exercise the CSIRP.

Define Your Assets. As mentioned in earlier chapters, your assets should be listed and categorized (such as business critical or key assets) to assist with decision-making during a significant cyber incident.

Hunt for Trouble. Here's where you detail how to identify and analyze a potential cyberattack. Establish a clear process for reporting and escalating suspected incidents. Outline investigative techniques for gathering evidence to understand the scope of the problem, and define processes for calling in third-party/external sources to assist.

Typically, organizations may call on their insurance at this point, once an investigation has deemed a significant event has occurred. But typically, escalations are sent to specialist external firms, such as incident response and digital forensics providers, and then supported by legal, public relations, and other specialists.

It should be noted that external parties will play a key role in providing advice to the board, to assist them in making decisions and overseeing the organization during a significant incident.

Also, ensure that you have defined evidence collection processes, and ensure you are keeping a detailed log of all activities, detections, and decisions with both dates and times, as this will be required by both external support providers, law enforcement and regulatory bodies such as the ACSC/ASD.

Communication. This is arguably the most important part of your CSIRP. Consumers in general do tend to be forgiving if communicated to well during an incident. People understand that breaches happen and really want to be in the loop, have some assurance around the organisations' security controls and activities performed now and into the future, and know what's next for them. On the same token, when a significant event happens, you may have various other companies or support providers involved such as media and PR firms. In general, you should designate a single person (or firm, e.g., PR) who will be responsible for communicating with external sources such as the media, as well as a designated internal contact for the rest of the organization. It is of extreme importance that in the event of a significant incident, these processes are in place, ensuring consistent, timely, and planned communication with external sources as well as internally. The messaging should be the same, and staff should not be communicating with the media or any other external sources, only referring them to the designated contact(s).

The communication from the organization should be designed to minimize reputational damage and will be frequent, accurate, transparent, empathetic, and responsive.

The CSIRP should also define how the organization will respond to regulators, as well as appropriate approvals for communication. You may need to disclose to the OAIC, ASIC, or any number of regulatory bodies. I'll flag again that if we take the OAIC NDB requirements, you only have 30 days to complete the end-to-end disclosure process from first detection, so a defined and structured approach will ensure these requirements are fulfilled.

It's also worth noting that directors of ASX-listed organizations have continuous disclosure obligations under the Corporations Act that require disclosure. If you are an ASX-listed organization, it is expected that you disclose cyber incidents and cyber risks as part of the operating and financial review process.

It is also recommended that even if you do not have any regulatory bodies that you need to report to, you still report the incident to the ACSC and to relevant law enforcement bodies.

As part of this phase, the organization should ensure they have a dedicated contact point for customers and organizations who may be impacted by the breach, as well as a web page set up to facilitate regular updates and communication with clients and the media. There should also be a defined process for handling customer queries and complaints, and if compensation or financial support is to be provided to customers, how they go about applying for this. The board should define and provide oversight of the above process.

Stop the Bleeding/Containment Measures. This section focuses on taking decisive action to halt the ongoing attack and prevent further damage. This might involve isolating compromised systems, revoking access for unauthorized users, or containing the spread of malicious software. This section should encompass supporting procedures and playbooks as well as cover evidence collection.

As cyber incidents can be quite fluid in nature, there should be a foundation/baseline for particular types of events, not set in stone, as specialist response firms may also be recommending actions and activities that will be fluid during an incident, depending on the TTPs utilized by the attackers. This section may also define resources and responsibilities for such tasks. These remediation plans should also have oversight of the board, in particular with regard to resourcing and capital expenditure.

Cyber Insurance Details. Within the CSIRP, the cyber insurance provider details should be listed (and accessible to everyone) as well as information on the level of cover and support available and what type of event and level would constitute engaging the insurance provider. Then documented processes and procedures should be in place to define how you communicate with the provider. It is recommended that a single person/ team be responsible for communicating with the insurance provider (as defined by your CSIRT).

Patch and Heal. The goal of this stage is to restore affected systems and data. It includes procedures for recovering lost data, managing and protecting backups, rebuilding compromised systems, and patching vulnerabilities to prevent future attacks.

The procedures in this stage should also define who is responsible for remediation activities, which resources, engaging third parties to assist, affected systems, and expected RTO (return to operation) objectives and how to monitor to ensure that no systems are still compromised.

It should be noted that in this recovery phase, the board may be required to facilitate additional short-term investment/capital for specialist providers and/or technology as well as facilitate a post-incident review, in conjunction with external firms such as incident response, forensics, and legal. This post-incident review should include an assessment of risk or harm (such as the OAIC NDB requirements) for impacted individuals or businesses and a review of all steps taken to prevent future occurrences.

It is a good idea to include in the plan what support is available to employees to ensure their ongoing well-being throughout the incident. It is common in large incidents (particularly high profile) that make the headlines that employees are hounded by media and reporters for information, as well as the toll it takes on IT teams and supporting managers during this process, with extensive work hours that may be involved, additional stress, strain on mental health, etc. It is important that the board acknowledge and support any initiatives to assist employees during this time.

Incident Notification and Reporting. The plan should define any relevant legal and regulatory obligations you have regarding data breaches or cybersecurity incidents. This section should also define:

- How to assess the incident for reporting obligations

- Type of incident/threshold that requires reporting

- Which agencies to report to, for example, ACSC, OAIC, etc.

- How to contact them and the details

- Who is responsible for disclosure/reporting

- Required reporting requirements and links to reporting resources

Note that in this phase, you will also be required to submit the timeline of events and activities mentioned previously.

Lessons Learned and Improvements

The plan should also outline how to review the incident to identify lessons learned and to identify areas for improvement. This review should encompass:

- Root cause analysis and how effective the organization's incident response process was

- Is additional training required both for employees and for staff involved in the incident response process

- How effective external support providers were

- Was sufficient budget and resources allocated to the incident

- Could the incident have been prevented and how

- What worked well and what could we have done better

- How could we improve our response processes and the CSIRP

- Is our cybersecurity strategy still fit for purpose

Additionally, the ACSC has developed a PPOSTTE model for assessing of incident response. Further details can be found in the plan template [44]. It encompasses the following areas to reflect upon:

People	Roles, responsibilities, accountabilities, skills
Process	Plans, policies, procedures, protocols, processes, templates, arrangements
Organization	Structures, culture, jurisdictional arrangements
Support	Infrastructure, facilities, maintenance

Technology	Equipment, systems, standards, security, interoperability
Training	Qualifications/skill levels, identification of required courses
*Exercise Management *This only applies to exercises*	Exercise development, structure, management, conduct

The CSIRP is also a living document. The plan should also be tested and reviewed periodically to reflect changes in your organization's environment and the ever-evolving cyber threat landscape.

The CSIRP should also seamlessly integrate with your organization's existing emergency, crisis, and business continuity plans. This ensures a coordinated and efficient response across all aspects of your operations. Cyber is classified as an operational risk, the same as any other risk, and needs to be managed, as it's impossible to eliminate this risk completely.

7.5.6 Testing of the Plan and Refinement

Now with the CSIRP developed, it should be tested at periodic intervals to ensure it is effective in the current threat landscape and tested against current (and/or emerging threats).

How often should an incident response plan be tested? It depends on the organization and its risk appetite, for the most part one to two times a year. Some critical infrastructure organizations may require a more frequent schedule, and compliance also plays a part here, mandating the schedule in some instances.

A lot of organizations schedule this in line with disaster recovery (DR) schedules, for example, the DR test twice a year and the CSIR test twice a year. In my opinion, quarterly is better, and the incident response plan should incorporate a simulated tabletop exercise as well as an actual simulated event.

The event should change from test to test, for example, ransomware one test, network breach another, phishing campaign another, and should be based upon current threats being exploited in the wild.

External parties can also assist here in generating the event (tooling) and running the exercise, with results reported back to the board and other key organizational stakeholders.

Similar to the previous section, the organization should assess what worked, what didn't, and what could be done better for each test, and refine the plan accordingly. Periodic review should also include reviews of the CSIRT team as well as third parties and should reflect any recent organizational changes.

7.5.7 Real-World Example – Incident Response Plan Challenges

As mentioned earlier, an organization's incident response plan and response abilities are often a major challenge for most organizations. I am often engaged by the C-suite or a director to perform testing of an organization via a simulated attack, but without providing knowledge of this attack to anyone in the organization bar a single or few people. A financial services company engaged me to perform an assessment of their organization back in 2022 to perform just such a test and to "get in via any means necessary." Once I was in, I was to perform standard TTPs (techniques, tactics, and procedures) used by threat actors and to be as noisy as possible so that their incident response plan would be kicked into action. After a short period, I obtained my entry. This organization had a careers page via their website (like most organizations), which linked to an external recruitment platform. I assumed that once someone applies for a role, it sends a copy of the application (CV, cover letter, etc.) straight to the HR team for review via email (which I have seen frequently), and often these platforms are set up so that any emails would bypass email filtering to ensure successful delivery to HR. I configured an office document with a payload (what we call malicious shellcode) and submitted my application for one of their available roles. Within 30 minutes, an HR person had reviewed my application and opened the Word document (ignoring any prompts), providing me direct access on to their machine.

I started some very noisy internal network reconnaissance and exploitation attacks, gaining access to systems and data as I went. As predicted and after a longer than expected time, they kicked their incident response plan into play. There were so many issues: first, it had never been tested; next, only one person knew where this file was stored, and they were on leave on a tropical island somewhere without cell coverage. Once they found the plan, the contact details were out of date for key contacts, and it covered basics like ransomware and restoring from backups but not from sophisticated (what we call APT) style attacks. The IT team went straight into panic mode locking down things here, there, and everywhere and inadvertently shutting down primary business operations and functions for the business. They were losing money, big dollars, there were rumors galore within the business, there was no structure or plan from the IT team, and they were planning on burning serious dollars with all sorts of third parties which they did not cater for. Communication within the business to internal stakeholders was huge, constant, and a mess, constant emails and messages, jumping from one thing to another; messages were all mixed and full of "maybe this has happened," "maybe we do this," etc. – it was a diabolical mess.

At the end of day 2, the CEO had advised me that we successfully tested to his specifications and was pleased (and also not pleased) that we confirmed his biggest fears and that we were now to sanitize and leave the network and he was to action thereafter.

7.5.8 Resources and Funding

Another risk area is a lack of security resources and security funding. Planning for cybersecurity resources and capital should encompass:

- Hiring of dedicated or hybrid security staff and ongoing salaries.

- Cybersecurity staff development, for example, training, security conferences, etc.

- General staff training and phishing.

- Allocation for a cyber incident to engage third parties, such as incident response, extra staff costs (think overtime), etc. Within this allocation, you should also consider downtime costs, compensation costs, and repairing brand reputation damage.

- Cyber insurance costs.

- Security protective technologies – think firewalls, SIEM, network devices, etc.

- Security software subscriptions and tools, for example, threat intelligence, dark web monitoring, vulnerability scanning, and analysis tools.

- Cloud security controls and DLP solutions to prevent sensitive data exfiltration.

- Outsourced security providers (MSSPs), for example, a SOC and SIEM, virtual CISO services, etc.

- Penetration testing.

- Security audits/compliance audits.

Obviously, there will be a bit of crossover here; for example, you may wish to not hire dedicated security personnel but utilize external parties to fulfill the same requirement.

It is recommended, however, that you consider having dedicated security resource(s) or a staff member with a majority security role, who will act as the single point of contact and as your security champion for the organization, to promote cybersecurity, respond to queries, and provide security reporting to leadership.

Which begs the question, how much should a board allocate in their budget to cybersecurity typically and as a percentage compared to IT spend?

There's no one-size-fits-all answer to cybersecurity budget allocation. It depends on several factors specific to your organization as well as your risk profile.

Some of the variable factors include

Size and Industry: Larger organizations and those in high-risk industries (finance, healthcare) typically require more extensive security measures.

Data Sensitivity: Organizations handling sensitive data (e.g., customer financial information, healthcare records) need stronger security controls.

Existing Security Posture: Organizations with existing security infrastructure might need less upfront investment compared to those starting from scratch.

Compliance Requirements: Regulations in your industry may dictate specific cybersecurity controls, impacting budget allocations.

Security Maturity: Organizations with a more mature security posture might spend less as a percentage of IT budget compared to those starting from scratch.

Your Cyber Insurance Coverage: Depending on the level of cover and how much you have budgeted and allocated for insurance, an organization may need to allocate less to incident response and third-party budget allocations, if they have these third-party costs already covered under their cyber insurance.

If we look at the industry averages, unfortunately, there isn't a massive amount of data out there on security budgeting. Some studies suggest small and medium businesses (SMBs) allocate anywhere from 6% to 12% of their IT budget to cybersecurity. This percentage can vary significantly depending on industry and company size.

Recent reports from Forrester [45][46] identify anywhere from 25% to 40%, depending on the organization.

Gartner research [47] suggests an average cybersecurity budget increase of 13% year over year globally.

The best method is to not focus on a specific percentage but approach cybersecurity budgeting with a risk management perspective. Here's how:

Identify and Assess Risks: Identify the cyber threats your organization faces and then assess the potential impact (financial, reputational) of a successful attack.

Prioritize Controls: Based on the risk assessment, prioritize cybersecurity controls (preventive measures, incident response) that deliver the most value in terms of risk reduction, and offer the greatest return on investment (ROI).

Cost-Benefit Analysis: For each control, consider the cost of implementation and ongoing maintenance compared to the potential cost reduction from mitigated risks.

There are many cost estimation tools and cyber risk calculators online that can also help estimate cybersecurity costs based on your organization's specific needs.

If this is all new to you, start with a baseline – even a small initial investment in essential security measures like endpoint protection and staff training can significantly improve your security posture.

Then scale up gradually – increase your cybersecurity budget as your organization grows and your security needs evolve. And lastly, seek expert advice – consider consulting cybersecurity professionals to help you assess your risks and develop a cost-effective cybersecurity strategy.

It's important to remember that cybersecurity is an investment, not just an expense. Investing in cybersecurity can prevent costly data breaches and operational disruptions not to mention improve customer trust and ensure organizational cyber resiliency – the more you can allocate, the better!

7.5.9 Cyber Insurance

Cyber insurance is a key component of ensuring organizational resilience and offers a valuable safety net for organizations. Cyber insurance should be seen as complementing insurance to management liability (ML) insurance. With ML, typically, this is a cyber extension or cyber add-on to this existing insurance. In the event of an incident, however, it typically provides a limited scope and cover, which is why a dedicated cyber insurance policy is essential. These are the typical differences between the two.

Feature	Cyber Cover in Management Liability Insurance	Full Cyber Insurance Cover
Scope	Limited, often focuses on D&O liability and regulatory fines.	Comprehensive, covers a wide range of cyber risks and financial losses.
Purpose	Protects directors and officers from personal liability and some incident-related costs.	Protects the organization from financial losses associated with various cyber threats.
Cost	Typically lower cost due to limited coverage.	May have higher premiums due to broader coverage.

The key benefits of having cyber insurance includes:

<u>**Financial Protection**</u>

Coverage for Incident Costs: Cyber insurance policies can help cover a wide range of expenses associated with cyberattacks, including:

- **Data Breach Notification:** Costs associated with notifying customers and regulators about a data breach.

- **Forensic Investigation:** Hiring forensic investigators to determine the scope and impact of the attack.

- **Legal Fees:** Costs associated with legal defense and potential lawsuits stemming from the breach.

- **Credit Monitoring:** Providing credit monitoring services to affected customers.

- **Business Interruption:** Reimbursement for lost revenue due to system downtime caused by the attack.

Ransomware Payments: In some cases, depending on the policy, cyber insurance may cover costs associated with ransomware payments. (Note: This is a controversial aspect, and some insurers are moving away from covering ransom payments.)

Improved Risk Management

- **Incentivizes Security Practices:** The underwriting process for cyber insurance often involves a security assessment. This can incentivize organizations to improve their cybersecurity posture to qualify for coverage or obtain better premiums.

- **Access to Expertise:** Some cyber insurance providers offer additional services beyond just financial compensation. This might include access to cybersecurity experts who can help with incident response planning and risk mitigation strategies.

Peace of Mind

- **Reduces Uncertainty:** Knowing you have cyber insurance in place can provide peace of mind and help you navigate the complexities of a cyberattack with more focus on recovery.

- **Improves Business Continuity:** By mitigating the financial impact of an attack, cyber insurance can help ensure business continuity and minimize disruption to your operations.

Some important considerations:

Cyber insurance is not a silver bullet and should not be seen as a replacement for robust cybersecurity practices. It's crucial to prioritize preventative measures to minimize the likelihood of an attack and to reduce the impact of an attack.

Cyber insurance policies vary significantly in terms of coverage details, exclusions, and limits. Carefully review and understand the specific terms of your policy, and ensure this is documented in your CSIRP and risk management frameworks.

Cyber insurance policies typically have deductibles, which are the initial amount you'll be responsible for paying before the insurance kicks in.

It's also important to understand how insurers assess an organization's cyber risk profile when applying for cyber insurance. Some of the key factors they consider include security posture, risk management, business continuity and DR, claims history, company size, industry, and compliance requirements.

Lastly, often the chief financial officer (CFO) for an organization makes the final decision on how much to cover and how much to spend when it comes to cyber insurance. To ensure optimal cyber insurance coverage, the chief financial officer (CFO) should collaborate with C-suite executives and key stakeholders, such as the IT manager or head of IT. By understanding the organization's risk profile, as identified through penetration testing and vulnerability assessments, the CFO can make informed decisions regarding coverage limits, budget allocations, and policy scope.

Security Posture

Security Controls: The strength and comprehensiveness of your organization's security controls (firewalls, intrusion detection, endpoint protection, data encryption) play a major role. Insurers favor organizations with robust security practices.

Patch Management: Efficient processes for identifying and applying security patches to software and systems demonstrate a proactive approach to risk mitigation.

Data Security Practices: Measures taken to protect sensitive data, such as access controls, data loss prevention (DLP) solutions, and user activity monitoring, are crucial factors.

Incident Response Plan: Having a documented and well-tested incident response plan demonstrates preparedness to handle cyberattacks.

Risk Management

Risk Assessment: Having conducted a thorough risk assessment that identifies and prioritizes cyber threats specific to your organization is a positive indicator.

Cybersecurity Awareness Training and Phishing: Regular training programs and phishing simulations for employees, to educate them on cybersecurity best practices and identify phishing attempts, reducing the risk of human error.

Penetration Testing: Regular penetration testing shows commitment to proactive risk management.

Business Continuity and Disaster Recovery (BCDR)

Backup and Recovery Procedures: The effectiveness of your data backup and recovery procedures is crucial for minimizing downtime and data loss in the event of an attack.

Business Impact Analysis (BIA): Having conducted a BIA that identifies critical business functions and the potential impact of a cyberattack on those functions demonstrates a proactive approach to recovery.

Disaster Recovery Plan: A documented and tested disaster recovery plan outlining steps to restore normal operations after an attack is a significant factor.

Claims History

Previous Cyber Incidents: A history of previous cyber incidents can impact insurability. However, demonstrating how you learned from past incidents and improved your security posture can be mitigating factors.

Other Considerations

Industry: Organizations in high-risk industries (finance, healthcare) may face higher premiums or stricter underwriting criteria.

Company Size: Larger organizations may have more complex cyber risks, potentially impacting premiums.

Regulatory Compliance: Compliance with relevant cybersecurity regulations can positively influence insurability.

Cyber Insurance Coverage: The specific types of coverage requested (e.g., data breach costs, business interruption) will influence the premium.

7.5.10 Key Questions for Your Organization

- Do we have robust logging and monitoring capabilities in place to detect security incidents?

- Is our logging infrastructure scalable and capable of handling high volumes of security events?

- Are we using Security Information and Event Management (SIEM) or similar solutions to centralize and analyze security logs?

- Do we have threat detection capabilities to identify anomalies and potential attacks?

- Do we have a dedicated security operations center (SOC) or are we using a managed security service provider (MSSP) for 24/7 monitoring and incident response?

- Are we able to quickly identify the root cause of security incidents and contain them effectively?

- Do have an incident response plan?

- Have we clearly defined all roles and responsibilities and ensured that the plan is available both on and off-line?

- Does the plan define when and which third parties will assist our organization in the event of an incident?

- When was the last time the plan was tested and refined?

- Do we have cyber insurance?

- Is the amount of cover we have suitable?

- Are there any gaps in coverage, for example, ransom payments, and how have we mitigated or reduced risks where we may not have coverage?

7.6 Assurance and Compliance

This is my favorite section as I've devoted close to 20 years on the job performing penetration testing, security auditing, and security consulting and assisting with compliance audits.

Assurance and Compliance is exactly that; it is all about providing assurance to the organization that the systems they have are working, they are doing what they are supposed to, and that they are reducing organizational risk as well as confirming that the costs associated with the investment are worthwhile.

Assurance also verifies the effectiveness of organizational policies and procedures that tie in with technological controls.

If we talk about compliance, there is a bit of overlap here, in that it confirms the presence of and testing of, say, organizational policies and procedures but does not provide any real assurance to the organization of their security posture, unlike, say, a penetration test, which actively assesses controls, but compliance can be used to demonstrate sound cybersecurity practices, policies, adoption of frameworks, and the implementation of security best practices and complements penetration testing practices. You will notice as part of a number of compliance frameworks that penetration testing falls under these as a required action that needs to be completed each year.

The Assurance and Compliance pillar covers any periodic assessment of an organization's security controls and validates the effectiveness of such controls.

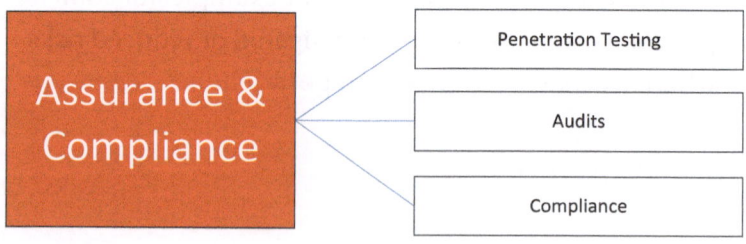

7.6.1 Penetration Testing

A penetration test (or pentest) is the method of actively evaluating the security of an information system or network by simulating an attack from a malicious source. During a pentest, a testing firm performs an assessment of your organization's security following a predefined methodology, from the position of a malicious attacker, to identify all of the risks, threats, vulnerabilities, and overall security posture for the organization, then tying those findings back to the operations of the business and risk profile, and then providing a report detailing those findings as well as recommendations to improve your security posture, thus increasing an organization's security posture, reducing risk, and providing validation of current security controls and practices.

Penetration testing usually encompasses all areas of a business during an engagement, such as users, staff awareness, security controls, policies and procedures, network hygiene, and deployment practices, but each engagement is typically tailored depending on organizational and compliance requirements.

Penetration testing is often completed by both internal testers to an organization and external providers; however, external providers are the only option that provides an independent assessment and satisfy compliance requirements.

At a super high level, this is what the pentest process looks like, and there's obviously a ton of tasks and particulars in between.

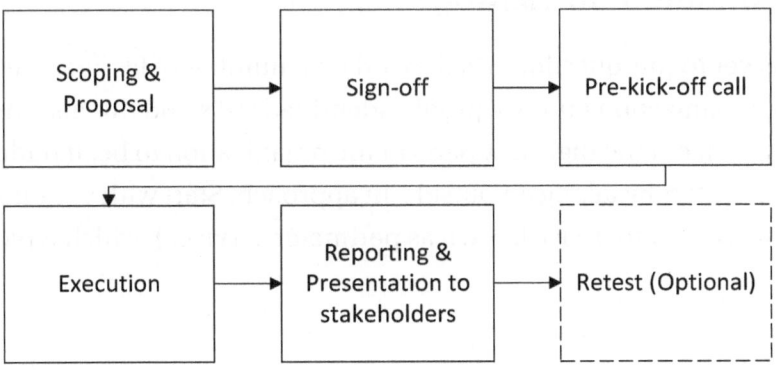

207

It's worth pointing out that penetration testing is not a silver bullet, and there is no guarantee that a penetration test will find every single possible issue in your environment or that you won't get hacked. It is a point in time assessment, based on a fixed amount of time; obviously, real attackers have all the time in the world.

Types of Penetration Testing

A penetration test can be one of three types:

Black Box: Tester has no information except the company name. Best simulates a real attacker, however, has the most cost associated.

White Box: Tester has full knowledge of the systems and/or internal access. This often is referred to as an internal assessment.

Gray Box: Most organizations opt for a gray box assessment. In a gray box assessment, an organization will provide some pieces of information to assist the tester, such as IP addresses; however, the engagement is largely the same as a black box but with reduced costs as the reconnaissance time is reduced due to this information being provided.

What Should I Be Testing?

The answer to this question will depend on a number of factors, such as budget, organization and risk profile, identified risks and threats, and where you deem the high-risk parts of the organization to be. If budget is a constraint, start by taking an outside-in approach. Start with your Internet-facing services (otherwise known as perimeter services), which typically include anything publicly facing like firewalls, VPNs, remote access services, web servers, etc. The perimeter testing should include testing (or at a minimum attacks) against cloud services like M365 and G-Suite and also reconnaissance of publicly facing information, such as compromised accounts, network infrastructure, cloud buckets, email addresses, and social media enumeration. The other focus area should be the end users with some social engineering attacks like phishing launched to obtain a picture of the level of awareness across the organization.

Also recommended in your phase 1 would be what we refer to as a breach simulation exercise (or assume breach testing). In this testing, your organization would provide a simulated entry point within the network and an account (mimicking a standard user), and the tester would then assess the available options to move laterally within the network, bypass controls, and elevate privileges. This type of testing best simulates a successful phishing attack.

Phase 2 would typically involve assessing other areas, such as an internal assessment of systems behind your firewall, testing of internal connected networks such as cloud infrastructure and wireless networks, and potentially examining your website or other web applications facing the Internet or any APIs in use for mobile applications (mobile apps). It obviously depends on your business model and functions; for example, if your main solution for customers is a web-based application or portal that they access, it makes sense to do this as part of the first phase.

Other components you may wish to include in phase 2 would be other social engineering attacks, such as vishing or smishing, physical access testing, USB drops, a password audit, or M365 review or assessment of other internal controls such as the workstation build, DLP controls, data exfiltration methods, etc.

To explain it in the concept of a standard corporate network, it would look like this:

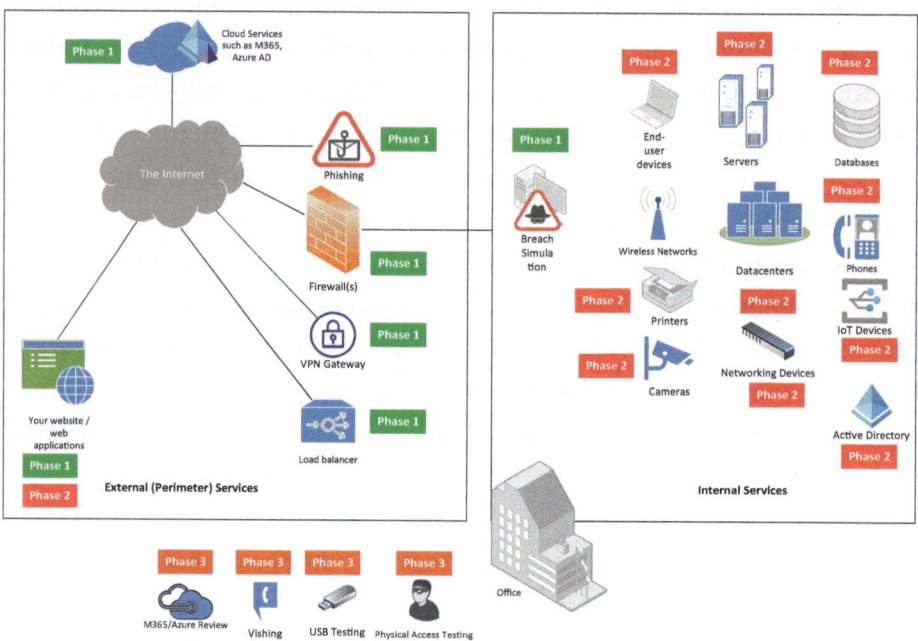

There is also nothing wrong with incorporating many or all forms of testing in one engagement and completing all of them right away to receive a complete picture across all risk areas of the business, especially if it's your first engagement and you are trying to get a benchmark of the organizations security posture. But typically, these days, I see organizations breaking up large engagements and the testing to run over the course of the year, rather than all at once; that way they can focus on remediation activities for one area at a time, for example, perimeter and phishing in January and February, remediation in March and April, then internal network in May, remediation in June and July, wireless in August, etc.

Then there is retesting; most testing organizations will provide the option or include a retest as standard, which is basically retesting of any discovered vulnerabilities after remediation efforts have been completed by the organization.

For more advanced organizations, they may engage a penetration test to encompass a red team assessment or a purple team assessment. A red team assessment involves the testing of various techniques and tactics, often utilizing many testers at the same time, whereas a purple team assessment is where a testing firm will work with an organization's internal or external security team (what we call a blue team) to launch activities, and the blue team will identify if the attacks are detected and stopped; basically, this is used to improve security team detection and response capabilities.

How Often Should I Be Performing Testing?

This again depends on your industry and risk profile. For most organizations, once a year is sufficient; however, you may have compliance requirements that dictate additional requirements. Most critical infrastructure clients that I work with perform biannual or monthly testing of systems.

Other factors that typically influence testing schedules are as follows:

Data Sensitivity: The more sensitive the data you handle (e.g., financial information, healthcare records), the more frequent testing is recommended.

Criticality of Systems: If a system outage would significantly disrupt your operations (e.g., online banking platform, ecommerce website), more frequent testing is advisable.

Regulatory Requirements: While not mandated in most cases, some regulations in your industry might indirectly influence testing frequency.

Changes to Your Environment: Any significant changes to your network infrastructure, applications, or security posture warrant a new penetration test.

Identified Vulnerabilities: If previous tests identified vulnerabilities, more frequent testing might be necessary to ensure remediation effectiveness.

For most organizations, there is a standard schedule of testing and audits that happen annually. These best practices typically involve an annual pentest, annual auditing for compliance (think ISO, PCI DSS, etc.), and, in-between this testing, monthly phishing and training of staff (all months), monthly vulnerability scanning, periodic internal reviews, and housekeeping. It may look similar to this:

January	February
January	
Penetration Test	**February**
Phishing simulation email to staff	Phishing simulation email to staff
Training of staff	Training of staff
Scheduled Vulnerability Scan	Scheduled Vulnerability Scan

March	April
March	
Housekeeping activities, internal review and cleanup, user accounts, data review	**April**
Phishing simulation email to staff	Phishing simulation email to staff
Training of staff	Training of staff
Scheduled Vulnerability Scan	Scheduled Vulnerability Scan

May	June
	Compliance Audit, PCI, ISO etc
May	**June**
Phishing simulation email to staff	Phishing simulation email to staff
Training of staff	Training of staff
Scheduled Vulnerability Scan	Scheduled Vulnerability Scan

July	August
July	
Housekeeping activities, internal review and cleanup, user accounts, data review	**August**
Phishing simulation email to staff	Phishing simulation email to staff
Training of staff	Training of staff
Scheduled Vulnerability Scan	Scheduled Vulnerability Scan

September	October
	October
	Housekeeping activities, internal review and cleanup, user accounts, data review
September	
Phishing simulation email to staff	Phishing simulation email to staff
Training of staff	Training of staff
Scheduled Vulnerability Scan	Scheduled Vulnerability Scan

November	December
November	
Additional Compliance Audit, e.g FIRB, APRA etc.	**December**
	Other internal reviews/audits
Phishing simulation email to staff	Phishing simulation email to staff
Training of staff	Training of staff
Scheduled Vulnerability Scan	Scheduled Vulnerability Scan

What Should I Be Looking for in Choosing a Penetration Testing Firm?

There are a myriad of penetration testing firms out there. Often a lot of testing firms follow the same processes and have similar proposals and costings, so it can be a challenge for management and directors to decide which vendor to select.

As a best practice, you should rotate vendors periodically to ensure that you are getting assessed via a different lens. On that note, if you are sticking to one vendor for multiple cycles, you should request that they rotate testers for each engagement to provide some form of different optics across your environment.

Factors to consider when selecting a vendor include the following.

Experience and Certifications

You should opt for organizations that are long standing and have worked with all areas and industries. Many organizations have testers that are a jack-of-all-trades, in that they can do all types of testing but are not specifically specialists in one area or the other. It is recommended that you consider adopting a firm that has specialist testers in certain areas, for example, a web application specialist who will be working on your website/webapp, a network specialist tester who will be working on your perimeter and internal, etc. When I refer to specialist tester, I'm referring to testers who work in one area of testing only, or for the majority of their engagements.

Similarly, certifications also play a part here. All testers should be police checked and vetted and hold certifications from industry bodies such as Offensive Security, CREST, TCM, and Altered Security. Common certifications include OSCP, OSCE, CREST CRT and INF, PNPT, and CRTP.

Certifications confirm that a tester has the technical skills, but experience trumps certifications any day of the week. Some of the best testers I know with decades of experience hold little to no certifications.

Additionally, the organization should be certified and accredited. You should engage organizations that are CREST certified [48]. An organization that is CREST certified has had its processes, deliverables, methodology, and the organization in general independently assessed to ensure it satisfies a set of minimum standards required by penetration testing firms.

Testing Methodology

Testing firms often utilize a custom methodology encompassing industry best practices, such as OWASP and NIST, combined with their own testing methods. You should be confirming that they have a tried and true method of testing, which should comply with or encompass some of the following standards:

- OWASP Application Security Verification Standard (ASVS) [49]

- NIST SP800-115 – Technical Guide to Information Security Testing and Assessment [50]

- OWASP Mobile Application Security Testing Guide (MASTG) [51]

- Pentest Execution Standard (PTES) [52]

- OSSTMM (Open Source Security Testing Methodology Manual) [53]

And yes, it is perfectly fine to ask the firm to describe their testing methodology and approach!

Reputation and Reference Clients

I also recommend assessing the organizations' reputation for their testing services. Firms that have only recently started offering penetration testing services may be inexperienced with the particular risks, threats, and knowledge of the landscape and vulnerabilities that may apply to your particular industry, which is only obtained through experience. Larger organizations do typically stick to larger firms due to this point alone as they require testing to be performed by people with experience specific to their industry.

It's also worth asking the vendor to provide some reference clients who can vouch for their deliverables, approach, communication, and methodology. This is typically seen in formal RFPs (especially for local government bodies, such as councils) and for more experienced organizations. I think every medium to large organization has been burned at one point or another by a not-so-great vendor, especially with regard to deliverables (reports), which is why this is a mandatory requirement for most mid-to-large organizations these days. Asking for reference clients also ensures that they have experience in your particular sector and industry.

Approach

Next up is assessing the organizations approach. How do they execute from start to finish? What level of communication is in place? This component is all about getting a feel for their experience and to identify the amount of planning they put into an engagement, to ensure it is run smoothly, is executed effectively, and does not impact the BAU (business as usual) for the organization.

At a minimum, you should expect from the testing firm

- Pre-execution information gathering processes.

- Pre-execution meeting including an execution schedule.

- Regular communications, daily or weekly updates or as required by the client schedule.

- Critical advisory, if something is found that is super high rated, they should advise you immediately so that immediate remediation efforts can commence.

- Reports to be sent as draft with the opportunity for the customer to comment and advise of changes such as severities. (They may have other mitigation controls the tester doesn't know about as an example.)

- Reports are then finalized and sent through.

- Wash-out meeting or final presentation is held with key stakeholders.

Deliverables

This is where the rubber meets the road. The key deliverables from the penetration test are the reports as well as the findings presentation to stakeholders. It is common for organizations to request a sample report (or be shown a sample report) from the testing firm. Personally, I don't send out sample reports to clients, but I'm happy to (and very often do) schedule a Teams meeting and run them through our reports, so they can see the deliverables and give them the opportunity to ask any questions they may have.

I have seen countless examples of bad reports from other firms over the years, which are just spat-out vulnerability scan outputs that have been tidied up (we will discuss vulnerability scans extensively in future sections), so it's best to do your due diligence here. At a minimum, the reports should encompass:

- An executive summary, designed for nontechnical stakeholders, presented in layman's terms, which explains the findings, where the risks are to the

organization, how they benchmark against similar
organizations and industries, and how they would
remediate the finding, for example, configuration
changes, implementation of policies and procedures,
etc. The executive summary should clearly show
severities and classifications to make it easier for
the board and other stakeholders to understand the
findings.

- Positive findings – the report should present the good,
the bad, and the ugly and identify positive security
controls that are in place, which made the tester's life
difficult.

- Best practices – recommended security best practices
outside of specific findings to further strengthen the
organization's security.

- Technical findings, which should be benchmarked
against the organization's technical controls,
operations and functions, business model, and security
controls, to define the actual exploitability and risk of
a finding. The probability, impact, and access method
should also be provided. The finding should provide
a proof of concept, steps to recreate, and screenshots
of exploitation, as well as how it can be daisy-chained
with other methods (or TTPs) and attacks to exploit the
vulnerability(ies). The finding should also encompass
benchmarks against CVSS (Common Vulnerability
Scoring System) [54] and the MITRE ATT&CK
framework [55] (or OWASP for web applications) and
should provide information to detect the vulnerability,
links to the tools used, references for further
information, as well as detailed remediation steps.

- Appendixes, such as reconnaissance information or informational findings and methodology and testing information.

Here is an example of a "penetration testing report" finding, which was received by a client of ours from a different vendor, which is in fact just a regurgitated Nessus scan.

The report finding:

SSL Version 2 and 3 Protocol Detected:

A network reconnaissance scan detected multiple hosts with a vulnerable version of SSLv2 and SSLv3. The remote service accepts connections encrypted using SSL 2.0 and/or
SSL 3.0. These versions of SSL are affected by several cryptographic flaws, including:

- An insecure padding scheme with CBC ciphers.
- Insecure session renegotiation and resumption schemes.

An attacker can exploit these flaws to conduct man-in-the-middle attacks or to decrypt communications between the affected service and clients.

Although SSL/TLS has a secure means for choosing the highest supported version of the protocol (so that these versions will be used only if the client or server support nothing better), many web browsers implement this in an unsafe way that allows an attacker to downgrade a connection (such as in POODLE). Therefore, it is recommended that these protocols be disabled entirely.

NIST has determined that SSL 3.0 is no longer acceptable for secure communications. As of the date of enforcement found in PCI DSS v3.1, any version of SSL will not meet the PCI SSC's definition of 'strong cryptography'.

Hosts Affected:

```
192.168.1.248  192.168.1.230
192.168.1.251  192.168.1.39
192.168.1.252  192.168.1.204
192.168.1.221  192.168.1.198
192.168.1.205  192.168.1.200
192.168.1.182  192.168.1.194
```

Here is what the Nessus vulnerability scanner reports (they are identical):

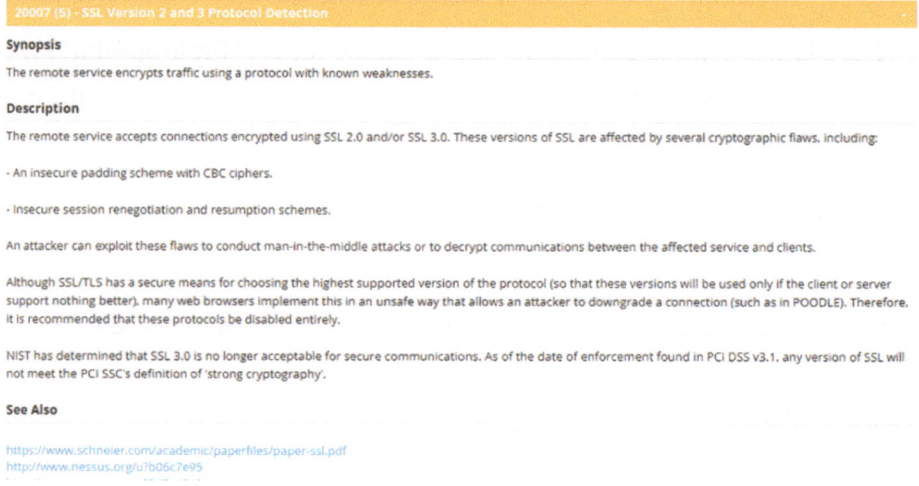

Here is what the text of the Nessus report reads:

20007 (5) - SSL Version 2 and 3 Protocol Detection

Synopsis

The remote service encrypts traffic using a protocol with known weaknesses.

Description

The remote service accepts connections encrypted using SSL 2.0 and/or SSL 3.0. These versions of SSL are affected by several cryptographic flaws, including:

- An insecure padding scheme with CBC ciphers.

- Insecure session renegotiation and resumption schemes.

An attacker can exploit these flaws to conduct man-in-the-middle attacks or to decrypt communications between the affected service and clients.

Although SSL/TLS has a secure means for choosing the highest supported version of the protocol (so that these versions will be used only if the client or server support nothing better), many web browsers implement this in an unsafe way that allows an attacker to downgrade a connection (such as in POODLE). Therefore, it is recommended that these protocols be disabled entirely.

NIST has determined that SSL 3.0 is no longer acceptable for secure communications. As of the date of enforcement found in PCI DSS v3.1, any version of SSL will not meet the PCI SSC's definition of 'strong cryptography'.

See Also

https://www.schneier.com/academic/paperfiles/paper-ssl.pdf
http://www.nessus.org/u?b06c7e95

Costs

Remember the old saying, "you pay peanuts, you get monkeys"? It's especially important when it comes to penetration testing. Most firms charge either daily or hourly rates; the cheapest option may not necessarily provide the best execution or deliverables, which is why they are cheaper than the rest. Typically, engagements are fixed price, and firms can also take a time-based approach, meaning they test as much as they can on that particular scope item until they are out of budget; this approach is often adopted by NFPs or organizations with very limited budgets.

You should opt for a firm in the mid-range ideally (budget is the deciding factor obviously), and if the testing firm ticks all your other boxes, but not costs, it is worthwhile approaching them to ask the best possible price they can do or, if the budget limit is a hard limit, to consider removing some scope.

How much to budget is difficult to quantify as it's dependent on a range of variables such as scope, after hours vs. business hours, on-site vs. off-site, the firm's testing approach, mandated requirements on the testing firm, and many other variables. I would allocate anywhere from $20k to $45k depending on size and budget. A typical $20k engagement would cover off all (if not most of) phase 1 items discussed previously, but also mentioned previously, rates vary sometimes dramatically from one vendor to the next, which is why you should be comparing quotes.

Comparing Quotes

You should ideally get two to three quotes to benchmark vendors, not just from a price perspective but also to assess their abilities, methodology, and approach.

Most quotations follow a standard process and layout, which includes

- Objective of the pentest or background information/ exec summary.

- Scope items/statement of work.

- Exclusions.

- Testing approach.

- Testing methodology information.

- Specific testing information associated with scope items.

- Deliverables.

- Pricing and effort.

- You may also see a section on retesting/revalidation of findings.

- Required actions/activities from the client's side and assumptions.

- Schedule of work (sometimes).

- Case study (sometimes, but rare).

- References (only if requested typically).

- Standard company information, such as marketing fluff on the organization and the testing teams, as well as information associated with confidentiality, IP, NDAs, insurance, data handling policies, and the testing firm's compliance status (CREST, ISO, etc.).

- Acceptance.

7.6.2 Vulnerability Scanning and Vulnerability Assessments (VA)

The next component in assurance and satisfying compliance is the use of vulnerability scanners and the performing of vulnerability scans.

Although this does fall under risk mitigation activities associated with the Technology pillar, I decided to put it under assurance as it does provide assurance of patch management related activities as well as flag the potential vulnerabilities that may exist within an environment.

Nearly all compliance requirements out there mandate the use of scanners and periodic vulnerability scanning. A vulnerability scan involves the purchase and deployment of a solution or product, for example, Nessus [56], which is then utilized to scan all assets within an organization for vulnerabilities. It will find all of the potential vulnerabilities that may exist across your assets, as well as validate patch management processes and configuration changes/lapses. These tools can also perform compliance-specific scans and testing against assets. Vulnerability scanning should be completed monthly as part of standard best-practice risk mitigation practices and findings remediated accordingly.

Pentest vs. Vulnerability Assessment

How does a pentest differ from a vulnerability assessment?

As mentioned previously, a lot of providers claim to be providing a "penetration test" at a reduced cost. In reality, though, they are providing what's referred to as a vulnerability assessment.

A vulnerability assessment is one component of the penetration testing process, but it only provides information on the "potential" vulnerabilities based on common findings, such as versions of particular software or registry keys.

There is no exploitation component to actively test if a "potential" vulnerability is a real exploitable vulnerability and usually does not encompass any other attacks that make up the breach process, such as targeting users, for example, phishing, passwords, exploiting the system, and seeing what can be done after the access has been obtained.

A vulnerability assessment normally does not encompass a reconnaissance phase as well. The Reconnaissance or Open Source Intelligence (OSINT) Gathering phase is used to gather pieces of information that are combined to create a network attack blueprint for an organization.

7.6.3 Security Audits and Compliance

Next up is security audits and compliance. These two types of assurance should be seen as complementing practices, and both are important aspects of cybersecurity, but they serve different purposes.

Security Audits

Security audits assess the overall effectiveness of an organization's cybersecurity controls. Audits aim to identify vulnerabilities, weaknesses, and potential security risks in your systems, networks, and processes. Examples include pentesting, vulnerability scanning, security posture assessments (SPA), Essential Eight audits, NIST audits, internal audits and data audits (executed by internal teams), security policy reviews, and awareness training assessments. The goal of audits, of course, is to provide a comprehensive picture of your cybersecurity posture and highlight areas for improvement. They help you prioritize security vulnerabilities and take corrective actions to strengthen your defenses.

So what benefit do security audits provide for the board?

Informed Decision-Making: By receiving insights from these audits, the board can make informed decisions about resource allocation for cybersecurity investments, prioritize security improvements, and ensure they are managing cyber risks effectively.

Improved Oversight: Regular security audits demonstrate a commitment to cybersecurity and provide the board with objective data to hold management accountable for the organization's security posture.

Enhanced Risk Communication: Insights from audits can be used to communicate cyber risks to the board in a clear and concise manner, facilitating better-informed discussions and decision-making.

Proactive Risk Management: By identifying vulnerabilities before they are exploited, audits enable a proactive approach to risk management, minimizing potential damage from cyberattacks.

Communication and Transparency: Security audit findings can inform communication strategies with stakeholders about the organization's cybersecurity posture and its commitment to data security.

By combining audit results with other relevant information, the board can gain a comprehensive understanding of cyber risk and ensure the organization is adequately prepared to address potential threats.

Compliance Audits

Compliance audits, on the other hand, verify whether your organization adheres to specific security standards or regulations, for example, ISO, PCI DSS, FIRB, etc. They ensure you meet the requirements set forth by industry regulations, data privacy laws, and/or internal security policies. Compliance audits often involve reviewing documentation, policies, and procedures to ensure they align with the relevant standards. They might also involve testing a subset of controls to confirm their implementation.

So what benefit do compliance audits provide for the board?

Cybersecurity compliance audits, while not a complete picture of cyber risk, offer valuable insights for boards to understand the organizations' adherence to regulations and industry standards, including identifying regulatory gaps and demonstrating due diligence and oversight. This includes:

Compliance with Specific Standards: Compliance audits ensure your organization meets the minimum security requirements set forth by external regulations (e.g., PCI DSS, ISO, GDPR, etc.). This helps the board understand areas where noncompliance could expose the organization to potential fines or penalties.

Prioritizing Resources: By highlighting areas of noncompliance, the board can prioritize resources to address those gaps and ensure adherence to regulations. This mitigates legal and financial risks associated with noncompliance.

Evidence of Compliance Efforts: A successful compliance audit demonstrates that the board is actively overseeing cybersecurity and taking steps to comply with relevant regulations. This can be crucial for improving the organization's public image and maintaining stakeholder trust.

There are of course limitations associated with compliance audits; for example, compliance audits focus on minimum requirements. They only verify adherence to specific standards, not the overall effectiveness of your security controls and the overall security posture of the organization. They obviously will not reveal all potential vulnerabilities that attackers could exploit.

Compliance audits also have a limited scope and may not cover all aspects of cybersecurity, potentially leaving blind spots in the board's understanding of the broader cyber risk landscape.

So while compliance audits are valuable, the board shouldn't solely rely on them to understand cyber risk. To obtain a more comprehensive picture:

Combine with Security Audits: Complementing compliance audits with broader security audits (e.g., penetration testing, vulnerability assessments) provides a more holistic view of your vulnerabilities and overall security posture.

Focus on Risk Management: Move beyond compliance to a risk-based approach. Understand the threats your organization faces, and prioritize security investments based on potential impact, not just regulatory requirements.

7.7 Key Questions for Your Organization

- Do we have a regular schedule of internal and external security audits to assess our compliance with relevant standards and regulations (e.g., ISO 27001, PCI DSS)?

- Are we performing monthly vulnerability scans against our assets and websites?

- Are we actively monitoring and addressing security vulnerabilities discovered through audits or vulnerability scans?

- Do we have a process in place to track and document evidence of compliance?

- Are we proactively identifying and addressing areas of noncompliance?

- Do we have a culture of continuous improvement in security practices?

- Are we using automated compliance tools to streamline compliance processes and reporting?

- Are we using security metrics and reporting to track our progress and communicate security performance to stakeholders?

- Are we adopting regular penetration testing?

- When was the last pentest?

- Were all the findings remediated?

- Does our penetration testing encompass all parts of our network, web applications, staff, and physical environment?

7.8 Key Takeaways

- Define your acceptable risk level (cyber risk appetite).

- Conduct regular risk assessments to identify and prioritize threats.

- Implement a layered defense with access controls, encryption, training, and detection/response.

- Foster a culture of security awareness through training and simulations. Educate employees on cyber threats and best practices.

- Continuously monitor and improve your security posture.

- Clearly define cybersecurity roles and responsibilities.

- Mitigate people risk with strong passwords, MFA, and secure IT practices.

- Address hybrid work challenges with secure devices and Zero Trust security.

- Implement standardized processes for IT hygiene and patch management.

- Conduct regular vulnerability scans and patch management.

- Maintain a comprehensive asset inventory and backup procedures.

- Leverage security tools like EDR/XDR, NGFW, and SIEM/SOAR.

- Develop a CSIRP plan for identifying, containing, and recovering from attacks.

- Regularly test and refine your CSIRP plan through exercises and simulations.

- Consider cyber insurance for financial protection and risk management.

- Combine penetration testing, vulnerability scans, and security audits for a comprehensive assessment, which provides a holistic view and to provide assurance.

- Move beyond compliance to a risk-based approach for optimal security.

References

[22]   www.aicd.com.au/content/dam/aicd/pdf/tools-resources/director-tools/board/cyber-security-governance-principles-web3.pdf

[23]   https://en.wikipedia.org/wiki/Deepfake#:~:text=Deepfakes%20(portmanteau%20of%20%22deep%20learning,not%20exist%20in%20real%20life.

[24]   www.esafety.gov.au/industry/tech-trends-and-challenges/
        deepfakes

[25]   https://danweis.me/_files/ugd/304557_589aa14f219b
        4e6690b125bec8b4ece9.ppt?dn=Security%20-%20Steve%20
        Riley%20-%20Defending%20layer%208%20-%20Social%20
        Engineering.ppt

[26]   https://query.prod.cms.rt.microsoft.com/cms/api/am/
        binary/RWJJdT

[27]   www.techtarget.com/searchsecurity/definition/identity-
        access-management-IAM-system

[28]   www.microsoft.com/en-au/security/business/security-101/
        what-is-identity-access-management-iam

[29]   www.microsoft.com/en-au/security/business/security-101/
        what-is-privileged-access-management-pam

[30]   https://pages.nist.gov/800-63-3/sp800-63b.html

[31]   https://docs.microsoft.com/en-us/azure/active-
        directory/authentication/howto-password-ban-bad-
        configure

[32]   www.cyber.gov.au/resources-business-and-government/
        essential-cyber-security/essential-eight/essential-
        eight-maturity-model

[33]   www.medibank.com.au/health-insurance/info/cyber-
        security/faqs/

[34]   www.afr.com/technology/revealed-how-hackers-used-a-
        tech-giant-to-get-inside-latitude-financial-20230323-p
        5cukr

[35]   https://thehackernews.com/

[36]   www.bleepingcomputer.com/

[37]   www.sans.org/newsletters/at-risk/

[38]   www.washingtonpost.com/politics/the-202-newsletters/
       the-technology-202/

[39]   https://packetstormsecurity.com/news/

[40]   www.microsoft.com/en-us/security/blog/

[41]   www.cyber.gov.au/resources-business-and-government/
       governance-and-user-education/incident-response/
       cyber-security-incident-response-planning-
       practitioner-guidance

[42]   https://view.officeapps.live.com/op/view.aspx?src=
       https%3A%2F%2Fwww.cyber.gov.au%2Fsites%2Fdefault%2Ff
       iles%2F2023-03%2FACSC-Cyber-Incident-Response-Plan-
       Template.docx&wdOrigin=BROWSELINK

[43]   https://nvlpubs.nist.gov/nistpubs/SpecialPublications/
       NIST.SP.800-61r2.pdf

[44]   https://view.officeapps.live.com/op/view.aspx?src=
       https%3A%2F%2Fwww.cyber.gov.au%2Fsites%2Fdefault%2Ff
       iles%2F2023-03%2FACSC-Cyber-Incident-Response-Plan-
       Template.docx&wdOrigin=BROWSELINK

[45]   https://go.forrester.com/wp-content/uploads/2023/07/
       Planning-Guide-2024_Security-And-Risk_.pdf

[46]   www.forrester.com/bold/planning-guide-2023-
       security-risk/

[47]   www.gartner.com/en/conferences/na/security-risk-management-us

[48]   www.crest-approved.org/

[49]   https://owasp.org/www-project-application-security-verification-standard/

[50]   www.nist.gov/privacy-framework/nist-sp-800-115

[51]   https://mas.owasp.org/MASTG/

[52]   www.pentest-standard.org/index.php/PTES_Technical_Guidelines

[53]   www.isecom.org/OSSTMM.3.pdf

[54]   https://nvd.nist.gov/vuln-metrics/cvss/v3-calculator

[55]   https://attack.mitre.org/

[56]   www.tenable.com/products/nessus

CHAPTER 8

We've Had an Incident

At this stage, you should be fully prepared for a cyber event; you have your documented incident response plan in place, it's been tested, and you know it works. You have implemented policies and procedures, adopted various security frameworks, and implemented technical controls; you have your due diligence covered, and you have a SOC in place monitoring the environment. But they still got in. It happens; sometimes emails manage to get through, sometimes the user provided the access, maybe it was a malicious insider, or a previously unknown vulnerability was exploited to breach your network. It happens.

When asked what is the number one piece of advice I could give to an organization that's been hacked? Stay calm. I know it is basic advice, but too often (especially with small businesses), they contact me in a panic, or their IT guys are in panic, not thinking straight, patching things here, there, and everywhere; it's a natural response when that "oh crap" moment kicks in, and then comes the flood of impulsive actions and responses when they get that first dreaded call from the negotiator stating "we have your data."

I have seen occurrences where businesses had an incident response plan in place for these types of events, and it wasn't tested, therefore didn't work, or was just put to the side in the heat of the moment. These things can't happen; a breach needs to be an expected and controlled event – the reason you invested all this time and effort was for this moment right now.

© The Editor(s) (if applicable) and The Author(s),
under exclusive license to APress Media, LLC, part of Springer Nature 2024
D. Weis, *Boardroom Cybersecurity*, https://doi.org/10.1007/979-8-8688-0785-5_8

So you assess the scenario, kick your plan into gear, and off you go. Whether your first step is to contact your cyber insurance company or to engage third parties after your initial assessment, it's important that when this happens, there is no blame game or scapegoating; cyber resiliency is a whole of the organization responsibility, not a responsibility of an individual or team, so you prepare as a team, then you respond, contain, and recover as a team, and then you learn from any mistakes along the way as a team.

If you do not have resources (and even if you do), the number you want to call is 1300CYBER1 for the ACSC who can help guide you and assist if you haven't had time to implement all the measures from this book and you have experienced a significant cyber event.

The AICD also has a great resource available via the website on the best governance practices for directors during a cyber crisis, available from here: `www.aicd.com.au/content/dam/aicd/pdf/news-media/research/2024/governing-through-a-cyber-crisis-280324.pdf`.

On a personal level, if you have been hacked or had your identity stolen, your first point of call should be idcare (`https://idcare.org`).

And lastly, don't forget your post-incident review to identify areas for improvement in the organization's cybersecurity posture.

8.1 To Pay or Not to Pay a Ransom or Extortion

I'll finish this chapter with a point on ransoms and extortion. Ransomware we know is prolific; it's seen in nearly every breach these days as well as extortion (which is the new norm). So should we pay? This is a continual question I receive from organizations.

The general advice and recommendation is to never pay a ransom or extortion; it continues to power the cybercrime ecosystem, and there is no guarantee you will get the data back or that it won't be disclosed at a later stage anyway.

If you or the board are considering a payment, it's best to seek expert external advice before making a decision and payment. It's not a one size fits all, and the board should assess the data loss impact, damage to operations and potential downtime, effects on customers and individuals, the backup and recovery options, the potential damage and/or loss of reputation due to the disclosure of the information taken, and the cost implications – there is a lot to consider here.

8.2 Understanding the Roles of Australian Agencies

There can often be confusion by organizations as to which agency they should be contacting when an incident has occurred. The golden rule is to report to the ACSC and the OAIC (if eligible under the NDBS).

Australia tackles cyberattacks, scams, anti-fraud efforts, and anti-terrorism through a well-coordinated effort between three key agencies. These are:

Australian Cyber Security Centre (ACSC): The ACSC serves as the national leader in cybersecurity, providing real-time threat assessments and guidance to both government and businesses. They coordinate national responses to cyber incidents, develop and maintain national cybersecurity strategies, and run the "Report a Cyber Attack" portal for incident reporting.

Australian Competition and Consumer Commission (ACCC): The ACCC prioritizes consumer protection and fair competition. They manage Scamwatch, a central hub for reporting and receiving information on scams. The ACCC investigates and takes action against scam operators, collaborates with the industry to disrupt phone and SMS scams, and works with telecommunication providers on initiatives like reducing scam calls and scam SMS messages.

Australian Federal Police (AFP): The AFP is the lead agency for federal law enforcement and national security. They investigate and prosecute cybercrime offenses, collaborate with international partners to combat transnational cybercrime, provide specialist cybercrime capabilities across Australia, and lead the Joint Policing Cybercrime Coordination Centre.

So in terms of who does what when an incident is reported, the ACSC acts as the central coordinator, disseminating advice and threat intelligence to all stakeholders. The ACCC focuses on consumer protection from scams and misleading conduct. Finally, the AFP takes the lead in investigating and prosecuting cybercrime offences.

8.3 The Executive and Board's Responsibilities During a Breach/ Significant Event

In the last section of this chapter, it's important that we explore the roles that the executive team and board play in the event of a breach. While the technical aspects of a cyber breach are crucial, they represent only a single thread in a complex web of consequences. Both the executive team and the board have critical roles to play in managing the fallout, far exceeding the realm of just IT.

A data breach triggers a cascade of legal investigations, public relations efforts, HR actions, operational disruptions, potential law enforcement involvement, forensic analysis, contract renegotiations, insurance claims, and financial losses.

The Executive Team: Leading the Response

The executive team will be responsible for:

Initial Containment and Assessment: The executive team spearheads the immediate response. This involves containing the breach, minimizing further damage, and initiating a forensic investigation to understand the scope and impact. Working with IT and security experts, they establish a clear incident response plan that outlines communication channels, reporting protocols, and containment measures.

Communication and Crisis Management: The executive team takes center stage in communicating with stakeholders. This includes informing internal teams, notifying potentially impacted customers, and engaging with regulatory bodies and law enforcement. Transparency and clear communication are critical to managing the crisis and minimizing reputational damage.

Operational Continuity and Recovery: Ensuring business continuity is a key responsibility. The executive team, alongside relevant departments like IT, operations, and finance, oversees the restoration of impacted systems and critical functions. They also collaborate with HR to address potential employee concerns and ensure appropriate training is provided post-breach.

The Board: Strategic Oversight and Accountability

While the board on the other hand is primarily responsible for oversight and long-term decisions, their role encompasses:

Providing Guidance and Support: The board plays a vital role in guiding the executive team's response. They offer strategic oversight, ensuring the response aligns with the organization's overall objectives and risk management framework. Additionally, they provide support and resources to ensure a swift and effective response.

Risk Management and Compliance: The board ultimately owns the organization's risk profile. Following a breach, the board reviews the effectiveness of existing cybersecurity measures and identifies areas for improvement. They also ensure compliance with relevant data privacy regulations and reporting requirements.

Long-Term Strategic Decisions: The board evaluates the long-term consequences of the breach and makes critical decisions. This may involve potential restructuring within the organization to strengthen cybersecurity posture, resource allocation for enhanced security investments, or even legal and financial considerations like potential lawsuits and insurance claims.

8.4 Real-World Example – Hollywood Presbyterian Medical Center

Hollywood Presbyterian Medical Center, a renowned hospital in Los Angeles, faced a harsh reality in February 2020. Hackers exploited a vulnerability in a third-party vendor's software, infiltrating the hospital's network. This breach wasn't a simple inconvenience. The attackers deployed ransomware, rendering it inaccessible. In Hollywood Presbyterian's case, this meant encrypting patient records, electronic health information, and administrative data. Effectively, the hospital's operations were crippled, hindering their ability to provide patient care.

Panic and confusion initially gripped the hospital. Doctors and nurses struggled to access patient records, delaying diagnoses and treatment. Management scrambled to contain the damage and isolate the infected systems. Fortunately, the hospital had a cyber insurance policy, which provided access to cybersecurity experts.

Working with their cyber insurance company and external security specialists, Hollywood Presbyterian activated their incident response plan. Restoring critical systems, especially those directly impacting patient care, became the top priority. This involved isolating infected systems, meticulously restoring backups, and patching vulnerabilities to prevent further attacks.

However, communication with patients and staff wasn't initially smooth. Many patients understandably felt frustrated by delays in treatment and the lack of information about their medical records. The hospital eventually issued a press release acknowledging the attack and outlining their response efforts.

The recovery process was slow, taking weeks to complete. While no patient data appeared to be compromised in this attack, some noncritical systems remained offline for a significant period. The disruption to patient care and the financial cost of recovery were substantial.

The Hollywood Presbyterian case serves as a stark reminder of the importance of the points raised in the chapter. Having a well-defined incident response plan, regularly testing its functionality, and maintaining clear communication with stakeholders are crucial steps in mitigating the impact of a cyberattack. Additionally, the reliance on third-party vendors underscores the need for robust security measures across the entire healthcare ecosystem.

8.5 Key Questions for Your Organization

- Do we have a well-defined and tested incident response plan that outlines clear roles and responsibilities for all stakeholders?

- Does our incident response clearly define communication protocols?

- Is the plan regularly reviewed and updated to reflect current threats?

- Are we aware of the roles and responsibilities of different stakeholders (executive team, board, external experts) during a cyber incident?

- Do we understand the importance of clear, timely, and transparent communication with stakeholders during and after a breach?

- Have we considered the potential financial, legal, and reputational consequences of a cyberattack and allocated resources accordingly?

- Are we prepared to make difficult decisions, such as whether or not to pay a ransom, in the event of an attack, and have we sought expert advice on this matter?

- Do we have a position on ransom payments?

- Do we have a dedicated incident response team or a process for assembling one in the event of an attack?

- Does the team have the necessary skills and resources to respond effectively?

- Is threat intelligence used to inform the organization's security strategy and prioritize controls?

- Are threat intelligence feeds from reputable sources integrated into security monitoring?

- Are sufficient resources and funding allocated to support cybersecurity initiatives?

- Is there a budget for incident response and recovery?

- Does the organization have cyber insurance coverage and is the coverage adequate for the organization's risk profile? Are the terms of the policy clearly understood?

- Do we have a process in place for conducting a post-incident review to identify lessons learned and improve our cybersecurity posture?

8.6 Key Takeaways

- **Stay Calm:** A cyberattack can be stressful, but panicking can lead to mistakes. Follow your predefined incident response plan.

- **Test Your Incident Response Plan:** Regularly test your plan to ensure it functions smoothly during a real attack.

- **Shared Responsibility:** Cybersecurity is a team effort. Everyone in the organization plays a role in preventing, responding to, and recovering from cyberattacks.

- **Seek Help If Needed:** The ACSC (1300CYBER1) can offer guidance and assistance in the event of a significant cyberattack.

- **Use Cyber Insurance:** Leverage cyber insurance to gain access to a network of specialists and professionals to assist with the event as well as to help offset costs associated with a cyberattack.

- **Legal and Regulatory Requirements:** Be aware of potential legal and regulatory reporting obligations following a cyberattack.

- **Communicate Transparently:** Clear and open communication with stakeholders (customers, employees, investors, media) is crucial after a breach.

- **Never Pay a Ransom Without Expert Advice:** Paying ransom fuels cybercrime and doesn't guarantee data recovery.

- **Assess the Impact:** Carefully consider the potential consequences of a cyberattack before making a decision on ransom payments.

CHAPTER 9

Understanding Penetration Testing Reports and Compliance Audits

A question I often receive from directors and boards is how to understand a penetration testing report or security audit, which is what we will cover in this last chapter.

9.1 Penetration Testing Reports

It's important to mention from the start that penetration testing reports and penetration testing, in general, are technical tests, and the reports are technical in nature, and often directors and the board require interpretation from the CIO, CISO, IT managers, risk management team, or anyone else that is overseeing pentests and cybersecurity for the organization. When this interpretation happens, sometimes the board may not receive the true picture of the level of cyber risk for the organization, and sometimes findings can be redacted as part of the interpretation to paint a more positive and cyber resilient picture of the organization.

The challenge with this is that directors and boards do not have the real picture of the organization's cybersecurity and cyber risk profile and the true level of the organization's cyber resilience. One way to minimize this challenge and to get assurance is to get the pentest firm to present the findings directly to the board (or provide a board-specific document), which is then unfiltered but requires the board to have a foundational understanding of the concepts explained in this book.

9.1.1 Understanding Scopes

The scope of a pentest can vary from engagement to engagement, and the terminology can change from vendor to vendor, and it can be difficult for directors to understand how findings map back to risks and actions. Typically, pentests encompass the following scopes and definitions, noting that different scope vulnerabilities may be chained together, leading to a more significant vulnerability overall, which requires faster remediation and response. For example, in a successful vishing call to a staff member, who provides their password to the attacker, the attacker then logs into the organization's network because of another finding, such as missing MFA; therefore, nothing is in place to stop them from connecting and accessing resources.

Scope Name	What's Being Tested	How It Increases Risk
• External Assessment	These are the IP addresses that are allocated to your organization from your internet service provider (ISP).	Vulnerabilities found here that contain a high CVSS score (we discuss CVSS in the next sections) are classified as high risk to the organization, as exploiting the vulnerability would effectively allow an outside attacker to potentially get access to, or affect your, protected internal networks.
• Perimeter Assessment	Think of this as any services you have that are facing the Internet and not protected by your firewall (effectively facing the outside world, outside of your network). This includes routers and firewalls (used for network connectivity), VPNs (virtual private network) which facilitate remote access from home into your corporate network, Outlook Web Access, and web applications for different technologies you use.	External vulnerabilities pose the most significant risk from people outside of your organization, and any findings in this scope should be remediated as a priority FIRST before remediating other scope findings.

(continued)

Scope Name	What's Being Tested	How It Increases Risk
• Cloud Assessment • M365 Assessment • Cloud or M365 Review	Testing of your cloud services, such as Microsoft 365 and Google G-Suite or systems you have that live in the cloud, for example, servers or web applications/ websites.	Vulnerabilities found here could be exploited to gain access to cloud services and the data that lives in the cloud, such as SharePoint, OneDrive, and Outlook data, or if we are talking about web applications, it may lead to an attacker gaining access to your customer data that lives in that web application, an example might be Salesforce or a CRM (Customer Relationship Management) system. Depending on how your organization operates and where you store your data, cloud-based vulnerabilities pose a significant risk (sometimes more than) compared to external findings. Findings here should be remediated as a priority. Remediate findings in this scope FIRST or SECOND before remediating other scope findings.

• Internal Assessment (Note that sometimes pentest firms put wireless findings under this category.)	This testing encompasses all of the devices inside your corporate network (think behind your firewall), such as servers, printers, network devices, user workstations, laptops, IoT devices, PLCs, or SCADA controllers.
	Findings in this area expose the organization to internal risks, such as malicious insiders or disgruntled employee threats, which allow internal threat actors' access to customer and other sensitive information that lives within the internal network.
	For an attacker to leverage or exploit vulnerabilities identified in this scope area, they need to be WITHIN the internal network already, meaning they need to have obtained an entry point into the network via a successful phishing attack or gained physical access to the office and breached the wireless networks, or where a user has plugged in a malicious USB or obtained another form of entry.
	It should also be noted that often supply chains and third parties may already have internal access to your network as part of the services they provide to the organization, so a finding on the internal network, where a third party has access to your systems, could also be leveraged from that third party's network as well.
	Remediate findings in this scope LAST compared to perimeter, social engineering, and cloud vulnerabilities/findings.

(continued)

Scope Name	What's Being Tested	How It Increases Risk
• Assume Breach Testing • Breach Simulation Exercise • Breach Scenario Testing (Note that sometimes pentest firms put findings in this area under the internal assessment category.)	This testing is where a tester has a simulated entry point onto a company-issued device/system, which has been provided to them by the organization. The tester then tests the available avenues to move throughout the network from this machine and what access to systems and data can be achieved. It best simulates a successful phishing attack or a scenario where an employee has disclosed their username and password to a threat actor and/or has provided that initial entry point we discussed under internal testing.	Findings in this section are the same as the preceding Internal Assessment section, in that they expose the organization to internal threats such as malicious insider or disgruntled employees, and are not as high risk as external, cloud, and social testing as the attacker would need to have that entry point provided to them in the first instance. Remediate findings in this scope per the internal assessment.

Phishing Assessment	Encompasses sending of phishing and spear phishing (malicious emails) to employees with the goal of stealing a user's password (credentials) or to coerce them to perform a malicious task, such as clicking of a link or opening an attachment with the goal of obtaining an entry point into the organization's systems or data repositories, for example, cloud storage locations.	Findings in this area are related to staff, and their lack of awareness, and are commonly remediated through employee training and phishing simulations as well as security culture changes.
• Spear Phishing Assessment		Vulnerabilities found here are classified as high risk to the organization, as exploiting the vulnerability would effectively allow an outside attacker to potentially get access to, or affect, your protected internal data and networks.
• Phishing Campaign		Findings in this area should be treated as high risk and remediated SECOND after external and cloud.
• Social Engineering Assessment		
• Social Engineering Campaign		
• Global Phishing Campaign		
• Targeted Phishing Campaign		
• APT Assessment		
• APT Campaign		

(continued)

Scope Name	What's Being Tested	How It Increases Risk
• Vishing (Note that sometimes pentest firms put findings in this area under the social engineering category.)	Encompasses calling up employees or connected third parties to try and convince them to provide sensitive information or to execute a malicious action, such as clicking a link.	Findings in this area are related to staff, and their lack of awareness, and are commonly remediated through employee training and policies and process changes as well as security culture changes. Vulnerabilities found here are classified as medium risk to most organizations, as exploiting the vulnerability would effectively allow an outside attacker to obtain access to sensitive information or potentially provide an entry to the attacker (if the user, say, followed through with clicking a link or what not). Findings in this area should be remediated THIRD after external, cloud, and phishing/social engineering.

• Wireless Assessment • WLAN Assessment	Encompasses testing of the wireless networks in use to identify if unauthorized access can be obtained through attacks against the wireless networks, if eavesdropping (what we call interception) attacks can be carried out, or if the networks are misconfigured allowing guest people to connect and access production systems and data (they should be separated).	Findings in this area are typically associated with misconfiguration of the wireless networks or the access points that broadcast the wireless network that you then connect to. Findings in this area should be treated as medium-low risk and remediated THIRD or FOURTH compared to other scopes. As for an attacker to exploit any vulnerabilities/findings discovered, they would need to be in physical proximity to the wireless networks that are broadcasting within your office(s).

(continued)

Scope Name	What's Being Tested	How It Increases Risk
• Webapp Assessment • Application Assessment • Web Application Assessment	Encompasses testing of web applications (or websites) to attacks that may provide access to data that the application may hold or access to any back-end systems which in turn provide access to data in other systems or internal systems.	Findings for web applications can vary greatly depending on how the application is used and what data it holds (they are relative). For example, if your web application hosts all of your members' personal information, such as names, addresses, DOBs, and phone numbers, or processes payments for your organization, a high-risk finding here would warrant immediate remediation activities (above potentially all other scope findings) to remove the risk of possible exposure and harm to individuals. If you are a SaaS-based organization where your entire bread and butter is the web portal you provide to customers, then findings here would be potentially high-critical rated and again would warrant a swift response. Another example: If the web application is only presenting, say, staff training material and nothing more, then findings here would be considered low risk as successful exploitation by an attacker would only provide access to basic training that would not affect the reputation, trust, or customers of the organization.

• API Assessment	Encompasses test of web APIs. APIs	Similar to web applications, the risk profile here depends
• WebAPI Assessment	are used to transfer or read data within	upon the data that is accessible or transferred via the web
	two points; for example, your mobile	API.
	phone banking app you have installed	The more sensitive the data and the easier it is to exploit the
	may connect over an API to retrieve the	finding to access the data, the higher the risk and the faster
	back-end data and information on your	it should be remediated.
	account, which is then presented in your	
	app, or the API you have might pass data	
	from one system or web application to	
	another.	

(continued)

253

Scope Name	What's Being Tested	How It Increases Risk
• Physical Access Assessment • Office Access Test • Building/ Location Test	Assessment of your physical location to try and physically access the office environment or to determine if employees will randomly plug in USB devices they find within proximity of the office. Physical access typically involves masquerading as a legitimate employee or contractor or as a supplier such as an electrician, courier, etc., in an attempt to get access to restricted areas and plug in a device or access a user desktop.	Findings in this area are related to staff, and their lack of awareness, and a lack of knowledge or enforcement of internal processes (such as ID badge checking). Findings in this scope are commonly remediated through employee training and policy and process changes as well as security culture changes.
• USB Drop • USB Assessment	USB drop is exactly that; a bunch of USB devices are configured with a payload or something malicious, so that when inserted, they provide an entry point to the network or steal data, and they are then dropped (placed) in the proximity of organizational locations, such as offices and depots.	For USB drops, this is typically remediated through IT controls. Vulnerabilities found here are again relative (per the web applications), but depending on how far the tester got, these are typically classified as high risk to most organizations, as exploiting any vulnerabilities in this category would effectively allow an outside attacker to access the physical office environment (think potential theft) and obtain access to sensitive information or facilitate a later entry to the attacker (e.g., they plugged in a backdoor access device). Findings in this area should be remediated SECOND after external and cloud if included in the scope of work.

• Password Audit	Testing encompasses a review of the end-user passwords (and system passwords) used within the internal network to identify the level of risk from weak password usage and adoption (weak passwords are passwords that are easily guessed by attackers providing access to accounts).	Findings in this area are related to staff awareness and password controls implemented by IT and are commonly remediated through employee training, IT controls (e.g., blocking of bad passwords), and policy changes (enforcing minimum characters, etc.) as well as security culture changes.
		Vulnerabilities found here are classified as medium-high risk to most organizations, as exploiting any findings here could potentially allow an outside attacker to obtain access to sensitive information or potentially provide an entry to the attacker (if not protected by MFA as an example).
		Findings in this area should be remediated SECOND or THIRD after external and cloud.

(continued)

255

Scope Name	What's Being Tested	How It Increases Risk
• Workstation Assessment	Testing here typically involves assessing the setup employed on employee-issued devices such as laptops and desktops, with the goal to identify security misconfiguration that allows an attacker or malicious insider to elevate their access.	Vulnerabilities identified in these scope areas could be exploited to elevate access inside your internal network once an attacker or malicious insider has access to a desktop or user device.
• Workstation Configuration Assessment		
• Endpoint Assessment	DLP testing involves assessing the various methods that attackers can use to take data out of a network once an entry point has been established.	Findings in these areas are typically low rated as an attacker would need to have preestablished a way onto a user device or server and credentials to exploit the finding.
• DLP Testing		Remediate findings in these scopes LAST after remediating other scope findings.
• DoS Testing	DoS (denial of service) testing encompasses saturating systems (e.g., flooding) with requests or data, with the goal being to shut down a system or force it to stop functioning correctly. Lastly, an endpoint protection assessment encompasses testing of the Endpoint Protection Product (think antivirus) to ensure it is effective and detecting a range of different malware and attack techniques employed by attackers.	
• Endpoint Protection Assessment		

I've grouped these types of testing because they are not common in most standard engagements, and the offering of these services varies greatly from one vendor to the next.

- ICS Assessment
- SCADA Assessment
- IoT Assessment
- Control Systems Assessment

Testing in this scope area encompasses testing of devices associated with infrastructure (hardware) and manufacturing, for example, Process Logic Controllers (PLCs) that operate machinery, controllers that open doors or change temperatures, and IoT (Internet of Things) devices that can be performing anything from solar arrays to doorbells.

Findings here again are relative to your business function and operations; for example, if you are a critical infrastructure provider, then your risk tolerance would be lower to findings in this area as opposed to an organization in manufacturing.

Other fluctuating factors include redundant systems; if a finding is only exploitable on one system out of two or another can take over on the fly if something happens to one device, then this obviously reduces the risk profile and severity. The last fluctuating factor is the level of access. Are these systems accessible from the corporate internal environment where there are risks from phishing and social engineering, or are they on heavily restricted and on isolated networks where you need to have physical or special access to interact with them?

Findings in this area are typically remediated AHEAD of internal findings but AFTER external, cloud, and social findings. Typically, though, most of these systems run on isolated networks.

9.1.2 Understanding Authentication

We touched on authentication briefly in earlier chapters. There are two types of authentication that can be utilized during testing:

- **Authenticated Testing:** The tester has access to credentials (username and password) or another form of authentication to verify that they should have access, for example, a token, code, or pin, which has been provided by the client in advance.

- **Unauthenticated Testing:** The tester is testing without any credentials, effectively anonymous (AKA anyone can access at any time), and often referred to in reports as "anonymous authentication."

The following table explains the authentication types and where they might be used:

Authentication Type	Scope Items
Authenticated	Web Applications
	Web APIs
	Internal Assessment
	Assume Breach Testing
	ICS/SCADA/OT testing
	Workstation Assessment
	Password Audit
	M365 Assessment
	Wireless Network Assessment

(continued)

Authentication Type	Scope Items
Unauthenticated	Web Applications
	Web APIs
	Internal Assessment
	Perimeter/External Assessment
	ICS/SCADA/OT Testing

There are four types of authentication types that will be referenced to in pentest reports, which are a key factor in how penetration testers determine the level of risk a particular finding poses to an organization. These are:

External Authenticated: Can be exploited from outside of the internal corporate network from the Internet but requires credentials (a username and password).

External Unauthenticated: Can be exploited from outside of the internal corporate network from the internet but does *not* require any credentials (a username and password).

Internal Authenticated: Can only be exploited from inside the internal corporate network and requires credentials (a username and password).

Internal Unauthenticated: Can only be exploited from inside the internal corporate network but does *not* require any credentials (a username and password).

9.1.3 Understanding Severities

As mentioned previously, typically testing firms associate vulnerabilities with the CVSS system as well as their own assessment against your environment and the specifics they identify.

The Common Vulnerability Scoring System (CVSS) is an industry-standard method for assessing the severity of security vulnerabilities. It provides a numerical score (0.0–10.0) that reflects the potential impact of a vulnerability on your systems.

CVSS (v3) considers three groups of metrics (and an additional one optional) to generate a base score:

Base Exploitability (Exploitability Score: 0.0–10.0): This score reflects the ease with which an attacker can exploit the vulnerability. Factors considered include:

- Required privileges (e.g., administrator access needed)

- Attack complexity (e.g., simple exploit code readily available)

- Authentication requirements

Base Impact (Impact Score: 0.0–10.0): This score reflects the potential damage caused if the vulnerability is exploited. Factors considered include:

- **Confidentiality:** The impact on the confidentiality of sensitive data.

- **Integrity:** The potential for data alteration or modification.

- **Availability:** The impact on system availability and functionality.

Scope (Scope Subscore: 0 or 1):
This binary metric considers whether the vulnerability can be exploited to gain unauthorized access to other systems or data (often referred to as "privileged access").

To calculate the base score, a formula is used to combine the exploitability score and impact score to generate the final base score, ranging from 0.0 (least severe) to 10.0 (most severe).

These severity ratings are:

Low (0.0–3.9): Low potential for exploit and minimal impact.

Medium (4.0–6.9): Moderate exploitability and potential for some consequential impact.

High (7.0–8.9): High exploitability and significant potential for serious impact.

Critical (9.0–10.0): Very high exploitability and potential for severe impact, requiring immediate remediation.

Temporal and Environmental Scores (Optional):
CVSS v3 allows for optional temporal and environmental scores to be added to the base score. These scores consider factors specific to your environment and the current threat landscape:

Temporal Score: Reflects the availability of exploit code, public knowledge of the vulnerability, and vendor response (e.g., patches available).

Environmental Score: Considers the specific characteristics of your IT environment (e.g., security controls in place, value of assets at risk).

To see how CVSS scores are calculated you can use the CVSS calculator here: `https://nvd.nist.gov/vuln-metrics/cvss/v3-calculator`.

It's also worth noting that CVSS does not assess social engineering tactics like phishing, which can bypass technical vulnerabilities.

9.1.4 Putting It Together

So for all penetration testers, they should be utilizing a correct methodology to determine the final low, medium, high, and critical findings that you see in the pentest reports. The methodology is as follows:

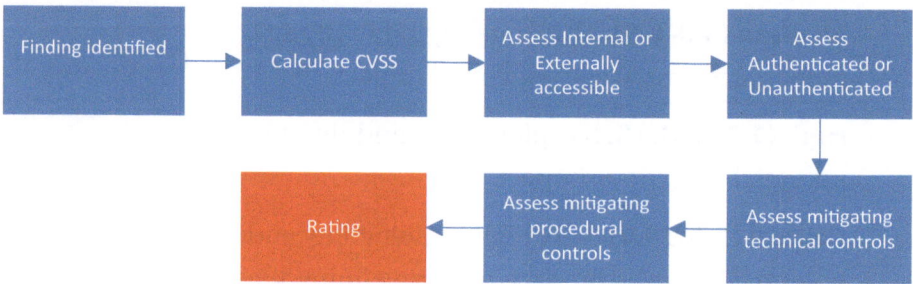

9.1.5 How Fast Should We Fix Findings?

This is another common area that fluctuates from organization to organization, and it's based on a myriad of factors, such as operational functions/requirements, mitigating controls, internal processes and procedures, risk appetite, change control processes and testing, IT schedules such as patching, and many many more.

If we take just the CVSS score (which as discussed previously there are several factors beyond CVSS), the severity and remediation are as follows:

Critical (CVSS 9.0–10.0): These vulnerabilities pose the most significant risk and require immediate attention. Patching or mitigating these vulnerabilities should be a top priority. Aim for remediation within hours or days.

High (CVSS 7.0–8.9): These vulnerabilities are highly exploitable and can cause serious damage. Strive to remediate them within a week or two, depending on the complexity of the fix.

Medium (CVSS 4.0–6.9): These vulnerabilities have moderate exploitability and potential for impact. Prioritize remediation, but consider the resource intensiveness of the fix. Aim for remediation within weeks or months.

Low (CVSS 0.0–3.9): These vulnerabilities are less likely to be exploited and may have minimal impact. However, they should still be addressed within a reasonable timeframe based on available resources. Prioritize patching these during routine maintenance cycles.

Additional Factors to Consider

Exploit Availability: If public exploit code is readily available, this will significantly raise the risk of exploitation.

Threat Landscape: Consider the current threat landscape and the prevalence of attacks targeting the specific vulnerability.

Business Impact: Evaluate the potential impact of a successful exploit on your critical systems or data. Higher business impact necessitates faster remediation.

Resource Availability: Balance the urgency of remediation with the resources required to implement a fix. Prioritize critical vulnerabilities even with limited resources, but consider a staged approach for addressing medium or low vulnerabilities.

Best Practices

- **Develop a Vulnerability Management Policy:** This policy should define clear timeframes for remediation based on CVSS severity and other relevant factors.

- **Prioritize Effectively:** Focus on addressing critical vulnerabilities first, followed by high, then medium, and finally low vulnerabilities within your set timeframes.

- **Consider Risk Management Frameworks:** Frameworks like the NIST Cybersecurity Framework [57] provide guidance on prioritizing vulnerabilities and allocating resources for remediation.

- **Continuous Monitoring:** Continuously monitor your systems for new vulnerabilities, and update your remediation plans accordingly.

CVSS is a valuable tool, but it's just a starting point. By considering the factors mentioned above, organizations can establish a risk-based approach to vulnerability remediation, prioritizing the most critical issues for their specific environment.

9.1.6 Understanding Exploits and Exploitation

Two common terms that you will see throughout a penetration testing report are exploits and exploitation. As mentioned previously, an exploit is a piece of malicious code designed to exploit a vulnerability or a hole in a system.

Many publicly available exploits can be obtained through various tools and frameworks, such as Metasploit [58], Exploit Pack [59], and Core Impact [60], as well as through sites such as exploit-DB [61], 0day.today [62], and SecurityFocus [63].

Exploitation is the act of utilizing an exploit to achieve a malicious goal, such as compromising a system, gaining access to data, or causing a denial-of-service condition.

9.1.7 Benchmarking

So how does the board benchmark pentest results from one year to the next (or one engagement to the next) to determine if they are improving or not? It is difficult even to benchmark at an industry level, as penetration testing results are not commonly disclosed for obvious reasons, leaving only cyberattacks and breaches as an industry benchmark. It is also worth noting that pentests also evolve in response to new and/or emerging threats, so comparisons on a year-on-year basis even within an organization may not paint a true picture.

Benchmarking Pentests

To benchmark pentests, you can utilize:

Number and Severity of Vulnerabilities: Track the total number of vulnerabilities identified in each pentest, along with a breakdown by severity (critical, high, medium, low). A decrease in the overall number of vulnerabilities, particularly critical and high ones, indicates improvement.

Note that this can fluctuate greatly though from year to year depending on which new vulnerabilities have been disclosed, what new systems have been introduced, and what new security controls have been adopted.

Exploitability of Vulnerabilities: Consider not just the number of vulnerabilities but also their exploitability. Focus on how easily attackers could leverage them to gain unauthorized access or cause harm. A decrease in highly exploitable vulnerabilities suggests improvement.

Vulnerability Retests: If specific vulnerabilities were identified in prior pentests, track whether they have been remediated by retesting them in subsequent engagements. A decrease in retested vulnerabilities demonstrates successful remediation efforts.

Time to Remediate: Track the average time taken to remediate vulnerabilities identified in pentests. A shorter remediation timeframe indicates a more proactive approach to security and faster patching cycles.

Note that to utilize any of the above, you will need to ensure consistency in the scope of your pentests year on year. Expanding the scope might reveal new vulnerabilities, making direct comparisons challenging, and in this instance, you will only be able to benchmark existing areas that are the same.

Some other areas to consider when benchmarking results are as follows:

Threat Landscape Changes: Account for evolving threats in your comparisons. New vulnerabilities emerge constantly, so some increase in vulnerabilities might be due to a more dynamic threat landscape, not necessarily a decline in security posture.

Security Maturity Model: Consider using a cybersecurity maturity model (e.g., NIST Cybersecurity Framework[64]) as a benchmark. Progressing through the maturity model indicates improvement in overall security practices, even if the number of vulnerabilities identified in pentests might fluctuate.

The limitations of pentesting for benchmarking are also worth mentioning:

- Penetration testing is a snapshot in time. New vulnerabilities might emerge after the pentest is complete.

- Pentesting methodologies can evolve. Changes in testing firms, testing methodology, and the assigned tester directly may affect the types of vulnerabilities identified, which can also affect year-over-year comparisons.

Effective Benchmarking

Combine pentest results with other security metrics. Look at security awareness training completion rates, phishing results, and incident response rates and times to get a more holistic view. Focus on trends over time. Don't rely solely on year-on-year comparisons. Track security metrics over a longer period to identify positive or negative trends in your overall security posture. Lastly, contextualize the results. Consider factors like changes in the organization's IT environment, new applications deployed, or industry-wide threat trends when interpreting the pentest results.

9.1.8 Mapping Pentest Results to Risk Reduction Director Duties

Directors of entities holding an Australian Financial Services License (AFSL) or those governed by the Corporations Act have specific duties related to risk management. Penetration testing results can be a valuable tool for boards to demonstrate how they are fulfilling these duties.

So how do a board and its directors then link pentest results to their director duties on risk reduction? Individual findings won't necessarily map to director duties, but penetration testing in general does, from both a duties and risk reduction perspective, for example:

Duty of Care and Due Diligence: Directors have a duty to exercise care and diligence in performing their duties. This includes understanding the organization's risk profile and implementing appropriate controls to mitigate those risks. Pentesting results provide an objective assessment of security vulnerabilities, helping directors fulfill this duty as well as showcase the board's awareness of cyber threats and their potential impact on the organization.

Duty to Prevent Insolvent Trading: Directors have a duty to prevent the company from trading while insolvent. Cyberattacks can have significant financial repercussions. Pentesting helps identify and address security weaknesses before they can be exploited, potentially leading to financial losses.

Inform Risk Management Strategy: The identified vulnerabilities can inform the organization's overall risk management strategy. By prioritizing and remediating these vulnerabilities, directors can demonstrate proactive risk mitigation efforts. Pentesting results also provide valuable data for the board to assess the organization's cybersecurity risk posture. The severity and exploitability of identified vulnerabilities inform the board of the potential consequences of a successful cyberattack.

Benchmark Progress: Regular penetration testing allows for year-on-year comparisons of vulnerabilities identified. This helps track progress in addressing cyber risks and demonstrates the board's commitment to continuous improvement.

Informed Decision-Making: Based on the pentest findings, the board can make informed decisions regarding security investments, prioritizing resources for remediation efforts and implementing appropriate security controls to mitigate identified risks.

Oversight of Management: Pentesting results can be used to evaluate the effectiveness of management's cybersecurity strategy and ensure they are taking appropriate actions to address vulnerabilities.

9.2 ISO 27001 Audit and Report Breakdown

An ISO 27001 audit is a review process that checks whether an organization's Information Security Management System (ISMS) aligns with the best practices outlined in the ISO/IEC 27001 standard.

There are two main types of ISO 27001 audits, an internal audit, which is conducted by your own staff or internal auditors to identify areas for improvement before an external audit, and the external audit, which is performed by an accredited certification body to determine if your ISMS meets the ISO 27001 standard for certification.

The reasons that organizations get certified are predominantly for customer confidence. ISO certification demonstrates a commitment to quality and standardized processes. This can boost customer trust and confidence in an organization's products or services and the other reason is for marketing and competitive advantages in certain industries, especially when bidding for contracts or tenders.

ISO 27001 is also obtained by organizations to meet compliance with regulations and industry standards.

Lastly, some contracts with third-party vendors or government agencies might stipulate specific information security controls. ISO 27001 certification can demonstrate that an organization has these controls in place.

It's important to note that achieving ISO 27001 certification is not a guarantee of perfect security but does show a commitment and ongoing process of improvement.

An ISO 27001 audit report is like a road map for your Information Security Management System (ISMS). It assesses how effectively your organization manages information security risks. It's typically made up of five sections:

Executive Summary

This is a high-level overview of the entire audit, highlighting key findings, including

- **Overall Effectiveness of Your Information Security Management System (ISMS):** Did it meet the ISO 27001 requirements?

- **Number and Severity of Findings:** Nonconformities, opportunities for improvement, etc.

- **Urgent or Critical Issues:** Any immediate risks requiring prompt attention.

- **Next Steps:** Recommended actions to address findings.

Scope and Audit Plan

This section outlines what was assessed during the audit, for example:

- Specific areas of the ISMS reviewed (e.g., access control, risk management)

- Locations and departments involved

- Reference to the ISO 27001 standard used

Previous Findings Results

This section outlines the remediation (corrective action) taken for the previously identified vulnerabilities from the last audit, for example:

Finding Reference	1465092-201704-N1	Certificate Reference	IS 600771
Certificate Standard	ISO/IEC 27001:2013	Clause	A18.1.1
Category	Minor		
Area/process:	Performance Monitoring & Measurement / ISMS Objectives / Compliance: 6.2, 9.1, A.18		
Details:	Legal and regulatory requirements not kept up to date		
Objective evidence:	REC 18 List of Legislation and Regulation v2.2 containing ███ legal and regulatory requirements was reviewed and it was noted that majority of the requirements were last reviewed in 2015.		
Cause	Incorrect version had been saved to the company ISMS as a document control error		
Correction / containment	Correct version was subsequently uploaded. Revision REC18.1A 0050728/0004 dated 08/02/2018		
Corrective action	Physical checks are now in place following system restores to ensure all current documents have carried forward as part of the restore		

Audit Findings

This is the core of the report, detailing identified issues. Look for three main categories:

- **Nonconformities:** These are deviations from ISO 27001 requirements. They can be major (critical system weaknesses) or minor (documentation gaps).

- **Opportunities for Improvement (OFIs):** These are areas where your ISMS could be strengthened, even if they don't violate the standard.

- **Observations:** These are informational notes about practices observed during the audit.

Each finding will typically include

Clause Reference: The specific ISO 27001 clause linked to the finding.

Description: A clear explanation of the issue identified.

Impact: How the finding might affect your information security posture.

Severity: Categorization of the nonconformity (major/ minor) or OFI (opportunity for improvement).

Finding Reference	1630565-201805-N1	Certificate Reference	IS 600771
Certificate Standard	ISO/IEC 27001:2013	Clause	7.5.2
Category	Minor		
Area/process:	ISMS policy and procedures, internal audits, corrective action. 5, 7, 9,10		
Statement of non-conformance:	Documents appearing in the live ISMS on the organization's intranet were viewed as being in draft format having not received formal approval from the Executive Leadership Team		
Clause requirements	Creating and updating When creating and updating documented information the organization shall ensure appropriate: c) review and approval for suitability and adequacy.		
Objective evidence	A number of documents within the ISMS on the intranet were noted to be in Draft format and had not been formally approved by the Executive Management Team. This is contrary to the organisations ISMS manual and was agreed with the guide.		
Cause			
Correction / containment			
Corrective action			

Finding Reference	1630565-201805-I1	Certificate Reference	IS 600771
Certificate Standard	ISO/IEC 27001:2013	Clause	A11.1.3
Category	Opportunity for Improvement		
Area/process:	Human Resource Security / Resource Planning. 7, A.7		
Details	Consideration to change the pin code for the key safe at regular intervals should be made. The current combination has not been changed for some time even though staff have left the department. There is still defence in depth around the information being protected hence an OFI and not NCR.		

Conclusion

This section summarizes the overall audit results:

- Confirmation of continued certification (if applicable)

- Reiteration of key findings and recommendations

9.2.1 Tips for Reading and Understanding an ISO 27001 Report

There is a lot of detail in an ISO 27001 report, and it's hard for directors to understand exactly what to look for and what key findings to pull from and action. In a nutshell:

Focus on Nonconformities: These are the most critical as they represent gaps in meeting the standard's requirements.

Evaluate the Impact: Consider how each finding could affect your organization's security posture.

Prioritize Based on Severity: Address major nonconformities and critical findings first.

Use the OFIs for Improvement: Leverage them to identify areas where you can strengthen your ISMS.

Develop a Corrective Action Plan: Outline steps to address each finding with timelines and responsibilities.

9.2.2 Benchmarking ISO 27001 Audit Results

Benchmarking is a little easier with ISO 27001 reports compared to penetration testing reports. Firstly, year-on-year re-assessment is predominantly a pass or fail – you achieved the standard or you didn't. It should be noted that once you pass the first assessment, it is much simpler to recertify each year after that.

Next, for each year, benchmark

- **Nonconformities (Major/Minor):** Deviations from ISO 27001 requirements.

- **Opportunities for Improvement (OFIs):** Areas for strengthening your ISMS.

- **Observations:** Informational notes from the audit.

Then compare numbers; compare the total number of findings (nonconformities, OFIs) across both years. Then identify trends in specific categories. Are nonconformities decreasing? Are OFIs focusing on new areas?

Another method can be to analyze the severity of nonconformities (major vs. minor) for year-on-year trends.

A reduction in any of the above would indicate an improvement in the organization's ISMS.

Lastly, you may wish to perform some qualitative analysis, for example:

Repeat Findings: Identify if any findings (nonconformities or OFIs) have reappeared in consecutive reports. This indicates unresolved issues.

Emerging Issues: Analyze if new types of findings appear in the latest report, suggesting evolving security risks.

Corrective Action Effectiveness: Review the effectiveness of corrective actions implemented from previous audits. Did they address the root cause of the issue?

9.2.3 Mapping ISO Audit Results to Risk Reduction Director Duties

The board has a fundamental responsibility to oversee and manage risk within the organization. An ISO 27001 certification process and its resulting reports can be a valuable tool for boards to fulfill their duties on risk reduction in cybersecurity, in particular

Nonconformities and OFIs: Findings from ISO 27001 audits (nonconformities and opportunities for improvement) directly translate to potential information security risks.

Board Oversight: By reviewing ISO 27001 reports, the board gains insights into the effectiveness of the ISMS in managing information security risks.

Proactive Approach: The focus on risk identification and assessment aligns with the board's duty to anticipate and proactively address potential threats.

Informed Decision-Making: ISO 27001 reports provide data-driven insights for the board to make informed decisions about resource allocation and security investments.

Accountability: The documented ISMS and audit trail create a clear record of the organization's efforts toward information security risk management.

Risk Mitigation Strategies: The board can leverage these reports to ensure the organization has appropriate risk mitigation strategies in place. This could involve

- Allocating resources for addressing nonconformities.

- Approving investments in new security controls identified by OFIs.

- Overseeing the implementation of corrective action plans.

Due Diligence

It also shows due diligence; the documented ISMS itself, established through the ISO 27001 certification process, serves as documented evidence of the organization's commitment to information security risk management.

Additionally, regular audits and their reports create an audit trail, demonstrating the ongoing process of identifying, assessing, and mitigating information security risks.

9.3 Real-World Example – Certified Yet Compromised: The TalkTalk Incident

A good example of how compliance does not equal security is TalkTalk, a major telecommunications provider in the UK that serves millions of customers with phone, broadband, and mobile services. In 2015, TalkTalk proudly announced achieving ISO 27001 certification, demonstrating their commitment to information security. This certification involved regular penetration testing and audits.

However, TalkTalk's approach to security reports had its shortcomings. Pentest reports, detailing discovered vulnerabilities, may not have been fully grasped by the IT team. The focus might have been on patching the most critical ones, leaving subtler vulnerabilities unaddressed due to a lack of understanding of the exploit scenarios described.

ISO audits, designed to assess the effectiveness of security controls, may not have gone far enough. While auditors reviewed documented procedures and interviewed staff, they might not have delved deeper to ensure that the implemented controls were truly effective.

This lack of in-depth understanding proved costly. A cyberattack exploited a seemingly minor vulnerability, one likely mentioned but not fully addressed in the pentest report. Hackers gained access to TalkTalk's network and remained undetected for a period, ultimately stealing the personal data of over 150,000 customers, including names, addresses, phone numbers, and some credit card details.

The breach triggered a public outcry, with customers questioning TalkTalk's commitment to security. The company faced significant regulatory fines and reputational damage. Investigations revealed a lack of understanding of pentest reports and a superficial approach to ISO audits.

A number of lessons were learned from TalkTalk:

Certification Is Not a Guarantee: ISO 27001 certification signifies a security focus, but it doesn't guarantee complete protection.

Invest in Understanding: Organizations must equip their staff with the knowledge to interpret pentest reports and implement effective remediation strategies.

Audits for Improvement: ISO audits are valuable opportunities to identify and address security gaps, not just compliance exercises.

Continuous Vigilance: Cybersecurity is an ongoing process. Organizations must continuously adapt their security posture based on evolving threats and incident lessons learned.

The TalkTalk incident serves as a real-world example of how companies with certifications and compliance can still fall victim to cyberattacks due to a lack of comprehensive understanding of security reports and a focus on compliance over true security effectiveness.

9.4 Key Questions for Your Organization

- Do we understand the difference between penetration testing and vulnerability assessments?

- Are we using a combination of security audits (penetration testing, vulnerability assessments) and compliance audits to gain a holistic view of our cybersecurity risks?

- Do we understand the different scopes of penetration testing (external, internal, social engineering, etc.) and their associated risks?

- Are we covering internal, external, wireless, and people as part of our scheduled penetration testing scope of works?

- Do we have a process in place to interpret and act on the findings of penetration tests and security audits, ensuring that technical details are translated into actionable insights for the board and management?

- Do we have a more general process for prioritizing and addressing vulnerabilities based on their severity (critical, high, medium, low) and exploitability?

- Are we using the results of these assessments to inform our risk management strategy and improve our security posture?

- Do we clearly define the scope and objectives of each penetration test, including specific systems, applications, or scenarios to be assessed?

- Are we engaging qualified and reputable penetration testing providers to ensure the quality and effectiveness of the assessments?

- Do we have a process in place to prioritize and remediate vulnerabilities identified during penetration testing, based on risk severity and potential impact?

- Are we documenting all penetration testing activities, including the scope, findings, remediation actions, and verification of fixes?

- Are we investing in training and resources to ensure our staff can effectively interpret and act upon penetration testing reports and audit findings?

- Are we conducting regular compliance audits to ensure that our security practices meet regulatory and industry standards?

- Do we have a process in place to interpret and act on the findings of compliance audits, addressing any identified gaps or deficiencies?

- Are we using the results of compliance audits to demonstrate our commitment to security and data protection to stakeholders, customers, and partners?

- Do we have a clear understanding of the specific compliance requirements applicable to our industry and the types of data we handle?

- Are we engaging qualified auditors to conduct independent compliance assessments and provide objective feedback?

- Do we maintain accurate and up-to-date documentation to demonstrate compliance with relevant standards and regulations?

- Are we incorporating compliance considerations into our overall risk management strategy and security program?

- Are we tracking trends in vulnerabilities, remediation times, and security awareness training completion rates to benchmark our security posture over time?

- Do we have a process for addressing ISO 27001 nonconformities (deviations from the standard) and opportunities for improvement (OFIs) identified in audit reports?

- Are we benchmarking our ISO 27001 audit results year over year to track progress and identify trends?

- Do we know how to benchmark penetration testing and ISO 27001 audit results to measure progress in cybersecurity?

9.5 Key Takeaways

- Penetration testing reports can be technical and challenging for directors and boards to understand.

- Request clear, unfiltered reports or presentations directly from the pentesters to gain a more complete picture of your organization's cybersecurity posture.

- Understand the different scopes of penetration testing (e.g., external, internal, social engineering) and how they map to potential risks.

- CVSS (Common Vulnerability Scoring System) is an industry standard for assessing vulnerability severity. A higher CVSS score indicates a greater risk.

- Prioritize remediation efforts based on vulnerability severity (critical, high, medium, low) and exploitability.

- Benchmarking pentest results year over year can be challenging, but tracking trends in vulnerabilities, remediation times, and security awareness training completion rates can provide valuable insights.

- Penetration testing results can be a valuable tool for directors to fulfill their duties related to risk management, due diligence, and preventing insolvent trading.

- ISO 27001 audits assess your Information Security Management System (ISMS). This system helps your organization manage information security risks effectively.

- The audit report provides valuable insights. It identifies areas where your ISMS aligns with best practices (ISO 27001 standard) and highlights potential weaknesses.

- Focus on nonconformities. These are deviations from the standard and represent the most critical findings requiring immediate attention.

- Benchmark ISO 27001 reports year on year. Track trends in nonconformities, OFIs, and their severity to measure progress in your ISMS.

- ISO 27001 certification demonstrates due diligence. The documented ISMS and audit trail serve as evidence of your commitment to information security risk management.

References

[57]   www.nist.gov/privacy-framework/nist-sp-800-61

[58]   www.metasploit.com/

[59]   https://exploitpack.com/

[60]   www.coresecurity.com/products/core-impact

[61]   www.exploit-db.com/

[62]   https://0day.today/search

[63]   https://bugtraq.securityfocus.com/archive

[64]   www.nist.gov/privacy-framework/nist-sp-800-61

APPENDIX A

Additional Resources

A.1 AICD Resources

Cyber Security Governance Principles Snapshot
www.aicd.com.au/content/dam/aicd/pdf/tools-resources/director-
tools/board/CCT-106-4-cyber-security-governance-principles-
snapshot-v2.pdf

AICD Cyber Security Governance Principles (Video)
https://vimeo.com/763250915/8496a1dd9b

Cyber Security Checklist for SMEs and NFPs
www.aicd.com.au/content/dam/aicd/pdf/tools-resources/director-
tools/board/CCT-106-4-sme-and-nfp-checklist-snapshot-v1B.pdf

Regulators Warn Directors to Step Up on Cyber Threats
www.aicd.com.au/risk-management/framework/cyber-security/
regulators-warn-directors-to-step-up-on-cyber-threats.html

Cyber Security Governance Principles
www.aicd.com.au/risk-management/framework/cyber-security/cyber-
security-governance-principles.html

Six Principles for Boards on Cyber Risk Governance
www.aicd.com.au/risk-management/framework/cyber-security/six-
principles-for-boards-on-cyber-risk-governance.html

A.2 ACSC Resources

ACSC: Main Page
www.cyber.gov.au/

ACSC: Cyber Assessment Tool
https://digitaltools.business.gov.au/jfe/form/SV_0dnd9cF15I8LnH
8?ref=acsc

ACSC: Cyber Reporting Portal
www.cyber.gov.au/acsc/report

ACSC: Questions for Boards to Ask About Cyber Security
www.cyber.gov.au/resources-business-and-government/governance-
and-user-education/governance/questions-boards-ask-about-
cyber-security

ACSC: Planning for Critical Vulnerabilities and Major Cyber Security Incidents – What Boards Need to Know
www.cyber.gov.au/resources-business-and-government/governance-
and-user-education/incident-response/planning-critical-
vulnerabilities-and-major-cyber-security-incidents-what-boards-
need-know

A.3 Other Cyber Security and Risk Resources

ISC2 Cyber Security Reports
www.isc2.org/research

Forrester Planning Guide 2024: Security and Risk
https://go.forrester.com/wp-content/uploads/2023/07/Planning-
Guide-2024_Security-And-Risk_.pdf

ASIC – Cyber Resilience Resources
https://asic.gov.au/regulatory-resources/corporate-governance/
cyber-resilience/resources-on-cyber-resilience/

NCSC Cyber Security Board Toolkit
www.ncsc.gov.uk/files/NCSC_Cyber-Security-Board-Toolkit.pdf

**Overview of Cyber Security Obligations for Corporate Leaders
(Australian Cyber and Infrastructure Security Centre)**
www.cisc.gov.au/resources-subsite/Documents/overview-cyber-
security-obligations-corporate-leaders.pdf

**World Economic Forum: How to prioritize resilience in the face of
cyber-attacks**
www.weforum.org/agenda/2023/01/how-to-prioritize-resilience-in-
the-face-of-cyber-attacks/

ASD Cyber Security Resources
www.asd.gov.au/about/what-we-do/cyber-security

Essential Eight Mitigation Strategies
www.cyber.gov.au/resources-business-and-government/essential-
cyber-security/essential-eight

Office of the Australian Information Commissioner (OAIC)
www.oaic.gov.au/

Cybersecurity Standards
www.standards.org.au/engagement-events/strategic-initiatives/
critical-and-emerging-technologies/cybersecurity-standards

National Institute of Standards and Technology (NIST)
www.nist.gov/cyberframework

MITRE ATT&CK:
https://attack.mitre.org/

Top Vendor Assessment Questionnaires: Including an ISO 27001 Questionnaire
www.upguard.com/blog/top-vendor-assessment-
questionnaires#toc-6-iso-27001-questionnaire

A CISO's Guide to Cybersecurity Disclosure & Compliance
https://go.gutsy.com/security-governance-whitepaper

APPENDIX B

Glossary

This appendix lists key terms you will encounter when discussing cyber risk, resilience, penetration testing, and security audits. At the end of this section are additional glossaries that can be utilized.

Access Control: Restricting access to systems and data based on user permissions.

Active Directory (AD): A directory service from Microsoft that stores information about network resources like users, groups, computers, and printers. It controls access to these resources and simplifies network administration.

ACSC Essential Eight: An Australian cybersecurity framework developed by the Australian Cyber Security Centre (ACSC) focusing on eight essential mitigation strategies to address common cyber threats.

Air Gap: A security measure that isolates a network from the Internet to prevent external attacks.

APEC Cross-Border Privacy Rules (CBPR): A non-binding framework for data privacy protection in the Asia-Pacific Economic Cooperation (APEC) region.

APRA (Australian Prudential Regulation Authority): The Australian regulator responsible for the prudential supervision of banks, credit unions, insurers, and superannuation entities.

ASIC (Australian Securities and Investments Commission): The Australian corporate regulator responsible for regulating financial markets, consumer credit, and investment activities

Assume Breach Testing: A simulated attack where the tester has a predetermined entry point on a device and tests how far they can move laterally within the network.

Attack Methods: Techniques used by cybercriminals to gain unauthorized access to computer systems or data. Examples include phishing, malware, and denial-of-service attacks.

Australian Energy Sector Cyber Security Framework (AESCSF): A framework for the Australian energy sector to improve cybersecurity posture and protect critical infrastructure.

Australian Government Protective Security Policy Framework (PSPF): A framework for Australian government entities to safeguard people, information, and assets through information security, physical security, and personnel security measures.

Authentication: The process of verifying a user's identity before granting access to a system or data.

Authorization: The process of determining and granting a user or system permission to access specific resources or perform certain actions.

Backdoor: A hidden method of gaining access to a computer system, often created by attackers to bypass security controls.

Benchmarking: The process of comparing your organization's performance against industry best practices or your own past performance.

Biometrics: Using unique physical or behavioral characteristics (fingerprint, facial recognition) for authentication.

Board Oversight: The responsibility of the board of directors to supervise the management of an organization, including its cybersecurity posture.

Breach Simulation Exercise: Similar to assume breach testing but may involve a broader scope and potentially involve social engineering techniques.

Breach: An incident where sensitive or confidential data is accessed and disclosed in an unauthorized manner.

Brute Force Attack: A trial-and-error method of attempting to guess a password by trying a large number of possibilities.

Business Continuity and Disaster Recovery (BCDR): Plans to ensure an organization can continue operations during and after a disaster or security incident.

Business Continuity: The ability of an organization to maintain critical business functions in the event of a disruption, such as a cyberattack.

Business Impact Analysis (BIA): An assessment of the potential financial and operational impact of cyberattacks on critical business processes.

Business Interruption: The disruption of normal business operations due to a cyberattack.

California Consumer Privacy Act (CCPA): A law in California that gives residents specific rights regarding their personal information held by businesses.

California Privacy Rights Act (CPRA): An expansion of the CCPA that grants California residents more control over their personal information.

CIS Controls: A prioritized set of best practices developed by the Center for Internet Security (CIS) to address the most prevalent cyber vulnerabilities. These controls are organized into six pillars.

Cloud Assessment: Testing of cloud-based services for vulnerabilities that could expose data stored there.

Cloud Controls Matrix (CCM): A framework developed by the Cloud Security Alliance (CSA) specifically designed to assess the security of cloud computing environments.

Cloud Security: Securing data and applications stored or running in the cloud

Compliance: Meeting industry standards or regulations to ensure data security and privacy.

Conditional Access: A feature in Azure Active Directory that allows organizations to control access to cloud resources based on predefined conditions. These conditions may include the device type, location, and user risk level.

Control Objectives for Information Technology (COBIT): A framework from ISACA that helps organizations govern and manage information technology (IT) effectively, with a focus on IT governance and best practices.

Corrective Action Plan: A documented plan outlining steps to address nonconformities and OFIs identified during an ISO audit. This plan should include timelines and assign responsibility for implementing corrective actions.

Critical Vulnerability: A vulnerability with a high CVSS score (typically 9.0–10.0) that poses a very high risk of exploitation and requires immediate remediation.

CVSS (Common Vulnerability Scoring System): An industry-standard method for assessing the severity of security vulnerabilities. It considers exploitability, impact, and scope to generate a score (0.0–10.0).

Cyber Resilience: The ability to withstand and recover from cyberattacks.

Cyber Risk Appetite: The level of cyber risk the board is willing to accept in pursuit of business objectives. Boards should define and periodically review their cyber risk appetite.

Cyber Risk: The potential for a cyberattack to damage an organization's systems, data, or reputation.

Cyber Threat: An attempt to gain unauthorized access to computer systems or networks or to disrupt or damage them.

Cybercrime: Criminal activity that targets computer systems, networks, and electronic data.

Cybercriminal: A person who commits crimes using computers or networks.

Cybersecurity Awareness Training: Educational programs for employees to educate them on cybersecurity threats and best practices. Boards should ensure adequate training is provided.

Cybersecurity Awareness: Educating users about cybersecurity threats and best practices.

Cybersecurity Ecosystem: The interconnected network of actors involved in cybercrime, including attackers, developers of malware, and facilitators of cybercrime activities.

Cybersecurity Framework: A set of guidelines and best practices for managing cybersecurity risks.

Cybersecurity Governance: The framework for managing and overseeing an organization's cybersecurity posture.

Cybersecurity Hygiene: Best practices for maintaining good cybersecurity habits, such as using strong passwords, being cautious about clicking links in emails, and keeping software up-to-date (Chapter 2).

Cybersecurity Insurance: An insurance policy that helps organizations cover financial losses associated with cyberattacks.

Cybersecurity Strategy: The high-level plan outlining how the organization will manage and mitigate cyber risks. Boards should be involved in approving the cybersecurity strategy.

Cybersecurity: The practices and technologies used to protect computer systems, networks, and data from unauthorized access, use, disclosure, disruption, modification, or destruction.

Darknet (or Dark Web): A hidden part of the Internet that is not indexed by search engines and requires specific software to access.

Data Breach Notification: The legal requirement to inform individuals and regulators when their personal data has been compromised. Boards should be informed of any potential breaches and understand reporting obligations.

Data Breach: An incident where sensitive or confidential data is accessed and disclosed in an unauthorized manner.

Data Loss Impact: The negative consequences of losing access to or control over data. This could include financial losses, reputational damage, and legal liabilities.

Data Loss Prevention (DLP): Technology that helps organizations prevent sensitive data from being accidentally or intentionally shared outside the organization.

Decryption: Unscrambling encrypted data back to its original form.

Denial-of-Service (DoS) Attack: An attempt to overwhelm a system with traffic, making it unavailable to legitimate users.

Digital Certificates: Electronic documents that verify the identity of a person or organization online.

Direction: The setting of cybersecurity goals and objectives by the board of directors.

Distributed Denial-of-Service (DDoS) Attack: A DoS attack launched from multiple compromised computers across the Internet.

Downtime: The period of time during which a system, network, or application is unavailable.

Due Diligence: Taking reasonable steps to ensure that an action or course of action is prudent and responsible.

Eligible Data Breach: A data breach that meets the criteria for notification under the NDB scheme. This means there has been unauthorized access or disclosure of personal information, and it's likely to result in serious harm.

Encryption at Rest: Secures data when it is stored on a device.

Encryption in Transit: Secures data while it is being transmitted over a network.

Encryption: Scrambling data to make it unreadable without a decryption key.

Endpoint Security: Protecting devices like laptops, desktops, and mobile phones from cyber threats.

Endpoint Protection: (Also called EDR) A software solution that protects devices like laptops, desktops, and mobile phones from malware, viruses, and other cyber threats. Endpoint protection typically includes features such as antivirus scanning, application whitelisting, and intrusion detection.

Executive Management Team (EMT): The team responsible for the day-to-day implementation of the cybersecurity strategy. Boards should receive regular updates from the EMT.

Exploit: A specific flaw or vulnerability in software that can be leveraged by attackers to gain unauthorized access to a system.

Exploitation: The act of using an exploit to gain unauthorized access or control of a computer system or network.

Extortion: The act of threatening to inflict harm unless a ransom is paid. In a cyber context, this could involve threatening to release stolen data if a ransom is not paid.

Firewalls: Software or hardware that controls incoming and outgoing network traffic based on security rules.

Gamification: The use of game design elements to make learning more engaging.

General Data Protection Regulation (GDPR): A regulation in EU law on data protection and privacy for individuals in the European Union (EU) and the European Economic Area (EEA).

Governance Principles: Broad guidelines that set the overall direction for an organization's cybersecurity posture. They address leadership commitment, risk management, and cultural aspects of security.

Gramm-Leach-Bliley Act (GLBA): A US law protecting the privacy of financial information held by financial institutions.

Hashing: A one-way function that converts data into a unique string (hash) that can't be used to recreate the original data.

Health Insurance Portability and Accountability Act (HIPAA): A US law safeguarding the privacy of individually identifiable health information.

Hybrid Working: A flexible work model that combines remote or home work with in-office workdays, allowing employees to split their time between different locations.

Incident Response Plan (IRP): A documented plan that outlines how an organization will respond to a cyber incident. The plan should include roles and responsibilities for different team members, communication protocols, and data recovery procedures.

Incident Response: The process of identifying, containing, and recovering from a security incident.

Insider Threat: The risk of malicious activity from within an organization by employees, contractors, or other trusted individuals.

Intrusion Detection System (IDS): Monitors network traffic for suspicious activity that may indicate an attack.

Intrusion Prevention System (IPS): Identifies and blocks malicious network traffic in real time.

ISO 27001: An international standard for information security management systems, outlining best practices for data protection.

ISMS: (Information Security Management System) A set of policies, procedures, and controls that an organization implements to manage the security risks associated with its information assets.

ISMS Manual: A core document within an Information Security Management System (ISMS). It outlines the organization's overall information security strategy and details how the ISMS operates.

Malware: Malicious software designed to harm a computer system.

Man-in-the-Middle (MitM) Attack: An eavesdropping attack where a malicious actor intercepts communication between two parties.

Maturity Model: A framework used to assess an organization's progress in implementing cybersecurity controls. It defines different levels of maturity (e.g., zero to three for the ACSC Essential Eight).

Metrics: Measurable data points used to track the effectiveness of an organization's cybersecurity program.

Microsoft Azure: A cloud computing platform that offers a wide range of services, including infrastructure, platform, and software as a service (IaaS, PaaS, SaaS). Organizations can use Azure to build, deploy, and manage applications without needing on-premise hardware.

Microsoft 365: M365 is a subscription service offering access to productivity software (e.g., Word, Excel, Outlook) and cloud services (e.g., OneDrive, Teams) for collaboration and communication.

Microsoft Entra: Microsoft Entra is Microsoft's new name for its cloud-based identity and access management (IAM) suite that offers a variety of services such as MFA and conditional access.

Microsoft Intune: A cloud-based mobile device management (MDM) service that allows organizations to manage and secure mobile devices like smartphones and tablets. Intune can enforce security policies, distribute apps, and remotely wipe lost or stolen devices.

Mitigation Strategies: Actions taken to reduce the risk or impact of a cyber threat (e.g., application control, patching applications).

Multi-factor Authentication (MFA): Requires users to provide two or more verification factors to access a system, improving security.

NIST Cybersecurity Framework (CSF): A voluntary, non-prescriptive framework from the National Institute of Standards and Technology (NIST) that helps organizations manage cybersecurity risks across five core functions: identify, protect, detect, respond, and recover.

Nonconformity: A deviation from the requirements of the ISO 27001 standard identified during an audit. These can be major (critical security weaknesses) or minor (documentation gaps).

Notifiable Data Breach (NDB): An incident where personal information held by an organization is lost, accessed, or disclosed without authorization, and this is likely to result in serious harm to one or more individuals.

OAIC (Office of the Australian Information Commissioner): The independent statutory agency responsible for overseeing privacy laws in Australia, including the Notifiable Data Breaches scheme.

Observation: An informational note from the auditors about practices observed during the audit.

Opportunity for Improvement (OFI): An area in the ISMS identified during an audit that could be strengthened, even if it doesn't violate the ISO 27001 standard.

Oversight: The monitoring of the effectiveness of an organization's cybersecurity program by the board of directors.

Password Cracking: The process of guessing or forcefully breaking a password to gain unauthorized access.

Patch Management: The process of finding, testing, and deploying security patches to fix vulnerabilities in software and systems.

Patch: A software update that fixes a security vulnerability.

Penetration Testing (Pen Testing): Simulating a cyberattack to identify vulnerabilities in a system and networks.

Penetration Tester: A penetration tester is an ethical hacker who simulates cyberattacks on a computer system or network with permission to identify vulnerabilities that malicious attackers could exploit.

Penetration Testing Report: The documented results of a simulated cyberattack, highlighting vulnerabilities and potential consequences.

Personally Identifiable Information (PII): Information or an opinion that can be used to identify an individual. This can include name, address, email address, phone number, date of birth, bank account details, and health information.

Phishing: A deceptive email or message designed to trick the recipient into clicking a malicious link or revealing personal information.

Phishing Simulations: Mock phishing attacks sent to employees to test their ability to identify and avoid real phishing attempts.

Post-incident Review: A process of examining a cyber incident to identify what went wrong, how the response could be improved, and what lessons can be learned to prevent future incidents.

Preparedness: The actions taken by an organization to prepare for and mitigate potential cyber threats.

Protected Health Information (PHI): Any health information that can be linked to a person. This includes medical records, diagnoses, treatment details, and insurance information.

Prudential Standards: Standards set by a regulatory body (e.g., APRA) to ensure the financial stability of institutions it regulates.

Ransomware: A type of malware that encrypts a victim's files, making them inaccessible, and demands a ransom payment to decrypt them.

Remote Access: The ability to access a computer system or network from a remote location, typically using a laptop, tablet, or smartphone over a secure connection.

Return on Security Investment (ROSI): A framework to assess the cost-effectiveness of cybersecurity investments. Boards can use ROSI to evaluate proposed security measures.

Risk Assessment: Evaluating the likelihood and potential impact of a security threat.

Risk Management: The process of identifying, assessing, and prioritizing risks to an organization. In cybersecurity, it refers specifically to risks related to cyber threats.

Security Controls: Measures implemented to safeguard an organization's assets, data, and systems from cyber threats. Controls can be technical (e.g., firewalls, encryption) or nontechnical (e.g., security policies, procedures).

Security Information and Event Management (SIEM): A system that collects and analyses security data from various sources to detect threats.

Security Metrics: Measurable data points that track the effectiveness of cybersecurity controls and the overall security posture of the organization. Boards should receive regular reports on key security metrics.

SOAR: (Security Orchestration, Automation, and Response) automates security tasks by coordinating tools, triggering responses based on playbooks, and managing incidents from start to finish.

Social Engineering: The art of manipulating people into revealing confidential information or taking actions that compromise security.

Spear Phishing: Targeted phishing attacks crafted to appear legitimate to a specific person or organization.

Standards: Documented specifications that provide a benchmark for good practice in a particular area (e.g., ISO 27001).

Standard Contractual Clauses (SCCs): Preapproved contracts for transferring data internationally under the GDPR.

Supply Chain Disruption: An interruption in the flow of goods and services due to a cyberattack, impacting delivery timelines, production, and customer satisfaction.

Supply Chain Visibility: Having a clear understanding of all participants in the supply chain, including their security posture, data flows, and potential risks. This helps identify weak links and potential security incidents.

Third-Party Risk Management: The process of evaluating and mitigating cybersecurity risks associated with vendors and other third-party partners. Boards should be informed of significant third-party risks.

Threat Intelligence: Information about cyber threats, attackers, and their methods.

Vendor Management System (VMS): A software system for managing vendor relationships, including security assessments and risk evaluations. This helps track vendor compliance with cybersecurity requirements.

Virtual Private Network (VPN): A secure tunnel that encrypts data traffic over the public Internet. It allows users to connect to a private network remotely, such as a company network from a home office.

Vishing: Phishing attacks conducted over the phone, attempting to trick victims into revealing sensitive information.

Vulnerability: A weakness in a system that can be exploited by attackers.

Vulnerability Management: The process of identifying, prioritizing, and remediating security vulnerabilities.

Vulnerability Report: A summary of identified vulnerabilities, their severity, and recommendations for remediation.

Vulnerability Scan: An automated process to identify weaknesses in systems and applications.

Webapp: A webapp (web application) is a software application accessed through a web browser, not requiring installation on individual devices, and delivering functionality similar to traditional desktop programs.

Wireless Access Points (WAPs): Devices that create a wireless network (Wi-Fi) connection. Users can connect their devices (laptops, phones, etc.) to the WAP to access the Internet or other network resources.

Whaling: A high-level spear-phishing attack targeting high-profile individuals within an organization, often for financial gain.

Zero-Day Exploit: A security vulnerability unknown to software vendors, making it highly dangerous until a patch is developed.

B.1 Other Glossaries

ACSC Glossary
www.cyber.gov.au/learn-basics/view-resources/glossary/a

UK National Cyber Security Centre (NCSC) Glossary
www.ncsc.gov.uk/files/NCSC_glossary.pdf

ISC2 Cybersecurity Glossary
www.isc2.org/certifications/cissp/cissp-student-glossary

SANS Institute Information Security Reading Room
www.sans.org/security-resources/glossary-of-terms/

Cloud Security Alliance (CSA) Glossary of Cloud Computing Terms
https://cloudsecurityalliance.org/cloud-security-glossary

Fortinet Cybersecurity Glossary
www.fortinet.com/resources/cyberglossary/guide

Palo Alto Networks Cybersecurity Glossary
www.paloaltonetworks.com/cyberpedia/cloud-security-glossary-faqs

Saylor Academy Cybersecurity Essentials Glossary
www.tufin.com/glossary-cybersecurity-terms

Cybrary Cybersecurity Glossary
www.cybrary.it/cybersecurity-glossary

B.2 Other Technology Glossaries

Techopedia: A comprehensive online encyclopedia with definitions for a vast range of technology terms.
www.techopedia.com/

PC Magazine Encyclopedia: A well-established resource for explanations of hardware, software, and IT concepts. `www.pcmag.com/`

Webopedia: Another extensive online dictionary dedicated to computer and Internet technology terms. `www.webopedia.com/`

Microsoft Docs: Microsoft provides glossaries and documentation for its various programm.ing languages and development tools. `https://learn.microsoft.com/en-us/docs/`

Index